We Used to Dance

We Used to Dance

Loving Judy, My Disabled Twin

Debbie Chein Morris

SHE WRITES PRESS

Published 2023
Printed in the United States of America
Print ISBN: 978-1-64742-573-9
E-ISBN: 978-1-64742-574-6
Library of Congress Control Number: 2023908615

For information, address:
She Writes Press
1569 Solano Ave #546
Berkeley, CA 94707

Interior Design by Kiran Spees

She Writes Press is a division of SparkPoint Studio, LLC.

Regarding the lyrics to "Look at Us, We're Walking," thorough efforts have been made to secure all permissions. Any omissions or corrections will be made in future editions.

Names and identifying characteristics have been changed to protect the privacy of certain individuals.

The conversations in this book are recounted to the best of the author's recollection.

To Judy,
my favorite dancing partner

and

To my children,
Ronen, Ilan, and Ari,
for whom I wrote this book

Contents

Prologue: We Used to Dance 1

Introduction: Judy. 3

1: Growing Up and Onward. 15

2: TNH: A New Life for Us All 30

3: Trying to Adjust. 40

4: The Visits Continue. 51

5: Mom 60

6: Pendulum. 66

7: Things Change, Anxieties Remain 75

8: Turmoil. 83

9: The Truth Comes Out. 91

10: Some Sunshine, Some Rain .101

11: Chairs, Candles, and Change. 111

12: Emotional Mayhem 120

13: The Storm Abates 133

14: It's Complicated. 141

15: The Pendulum Comes to a Halt. 150

Epilogue: Finding Peace 162

Prologue
We Used to Dance

The more time I spend on this earth, the more I see the impossibility of going through life without experiencing some sort of life-altering event—be it the death of a loved one, the diagnosis of serious illness, or a tragic accident. For my parents, it was the birth of their daughters.

We had spent nearly nine months together, my sister and I, cramped within that small space. And when the time finally arrived for us to enter the world, after positioning ourselves for our arrival, she dropped down in front of me and emerged feet-first, the cord wrapped around her tiny neck. That only added insult to the already existing injury; there was evidence that her cord had not been healthy, and she may have been deprived of oxygen even before that moment. Whisked away to intensive care and remaining there even after I was taken home, it wasn't clear if she would live to join me and our two brothers. But she did survive and, once she had stabilized, the doctors sent her home, knowing there was damage but unsure of the extent. Only time would reveal the answer to that question. And time, as it turned out, was not our friend.

We used to dance, my sister and I. There we'd go, swirling around the room, both of us laughing with glee. Of course, we were younger then; she, more relaxed and I, more able to hold her in my arms. Oh, how we dipped and glided, so comfortable was she in my arms. Those were happy days when we used to dance.

Introduction
Judy

My earliest memory is from when I was about two years old. I am cheerfully saying good night to my sister, standing at the head of my crib peering out over the top. Judy is lying on her stomach looking up at me from her own crib. Our cribs are perpendicular to each other, with a small night table between. Is it then or in later years that Raggedy Ann and Avis sit silently watching? Ann, which was not only the given name of the doll but also, coincidentally, my middle name, is my doll; Avis, Judy's middle name, is hers. Judy laughs as I say good night. In a few minutes, my father will sit in a chair between our beds and sing us lullabies. It is really for Judy, who does not fall asleep as easily as I, but I, of course, also reap the benefits. In later years, my father managed to slowly remove himself from this nightly task, first shifting his seat to the other side of the room near the door, then just outside the room, then down the long hallway in our apartment, until finally he was relieved of his duty. For many years, though, I benefited from my sister's need to have him nearby.

Another looming memory is not of an event or circumstance but of a photograph. We are younger than in my true memory—only about a year old or so. As in the true memory, I am standing, and Judy is lying on her stomach, looking up. We are in our playpen, both smiling happily at the camera. When I discovered the photo years later, though, it did not bring a smile to my face but rather a sadness that this is how it was and how it would always be: me, able and ready to meet the world; Judy, forever bound by her disability.

It took nine months until Judy was officially diagnosed with cerebral palsy (CP), which Merriam-Webster defines as "a disability resulting from damage to the brain before, during, or shortly after birth and outwardly manifested by muscular incoordination and speech disturbances." As Judy made her way from infancy to toddlerhood, it became apparent that she was going to have physical limitations, but in the beginning it was unclear how severe those limitations would be. At that time, infants were often placed on their stomachs, and it was from there that we learned how to roll over. Judy began lifting herself up with her hands before I did, and that was seen as a good sign. However, as it turned out, it was due to her muscle rigidity and did not indicate an ability to control her body. Long into our childhood, we played a game in which Judy would lie on her bed and lift herself up and up and up on her hands, until, ultimately, she tipped over. Depending on how she landed, she might pull her arm out from under her and be back on her stomach (and repeat the process), or she may have tipped over too far and now be in jeopardy of falling off her bed. That would cause her to laugh aloud, and someone would come running to her room to save her as she dangled precariously above the floor. But Judy always thought it was so funny!

Judy never had control of her hands or leg muscles, and, when she was young, she had limited control of one of her arms. When attempting to move the arm forward, she would first pull it back before extending it forward, although she was never able to extend it very far. Over the years, her increasing spasticity prevented even that. Never fully able to hold her head up on her own, she eventually needed one and then two head supports added to her wheelchair, and, for a while, she was able to move her head from side to side with that support.

Though she was severely disabled, Judy was able to do many things. She could breathe on her own. She could laugh, and she could cry. She was considered cognitively impaired, but she understood a lot of what went on around her. When she was ten months old, she ran a high fever and was hospitalized for about ten days. The cause of the fever was never found, but when it finally subsided, she was sent home. For years afterward, whenever we happened to pass by that hospital, Judy, looking out the car window, would start to cry. She clearly remembered it was a place she didn't like. In addition to her phenomenal memory, Judy understood when people spoke to her and responded through particular mouth motions: an opening and lowering of the jaw was "yes"; a sidelong grimace meant "no." She laughed when someone said something that amused her and made guttural noises indicating that she disagreed if she didn't like what you were saying or was unhappy about her routine being disrupted. Judy enjoyed listening to rock and roll music on the radio and to songs from Broadway shows on tape. Her favorite tapes were ones our family made for her, detailing a trip we had taken or a family story.

Her daily routine also included watching TV sitcoms and family dramas. She would scream when anyone yelled on *I Love Lucy* and cry when Lassie was lost, but she wouldn't miss an episode.

Every year, once a year, the Cerebral Palsy Telethon was on TV. We watched together from morning till night, with host Dennis James. Even after we grew older, and I no longer lived at home, Judy continued to watch. We also watched the Jerry Lewis Muscular Dystrophy Telethon—which, to my great frustration, always collected so much more money—but the CP telethon was by far our favorite. I don't know what she loved about it, but for me, for a long time, it signified hope. I watched as they brought out the children, and I ached—with joy for the child and with longing for Judy and me—when one of the children would throw away her crutches and walk, some, they said, for the very first time. And the special telethon song would be sung . . .

Look at us, we're walking.
Look at us, we're talking.
We who never walked or talked before.

Look at us, we're laughing.
   We're happy and we're laughing.
   Thank you from our hearts, forever more.

But there are so many other children,
   Who only speak with a silent prayer.
   For those who haven't been so lucky,
   We hope and pray you will always care.

And someday they'll be walking.
   Someday they'll be talking.
   Imagine walking to the candy store.

But the fight has just begun.
   Get behind us, everyone.
   Your dollars make our dreams come true.
   Thanks to you, thanks to you.

I knew that Judy was one of those *other children*, and I would sit and dream about us walking together to the candy store. For years, I imagined the two of us laughing as we headed down the street to Featherbed Lane to buy some candy. And I prayed. I prayed and I prayed and I prayed.

Sadly, there was no walking and no candy in Judy's future. Judy was never able to even *use* crutches, never mind throw them away. She also wasn't able to chew. She *tongued* the soft foods that my mother or grandmother—or I—fed her. She was able to swallow soft or pureed food, but even that often ended in bouts of coughing, with food spraying everywhere, much of it landing on the bib she always had to wear (to catch her drool as well as her food). Growing up, we had a parakeet we named Pee Wee. Pee Wee was the happy recipient of Judy's inability to keep food in her mouth until it was swallowed. He loved to fly around the kitchen, his favorite landing spot being Judy's bib. Pee Wee would alight onto Judy's shoulder or head and then walk down onto her bib, strolling up and down, pecking at the food bits that had fallen there. Judy loved Pee Wee and would laugh every time he visited her, clearly enjoying his foraging attempts.

Since Judy couldn't chew, her teeth weakened over time, and despite efforts to brush them daily (not easy because Judy wasn't able to keep her mouth open) and regular visits to the dentist, they soon began to decay. Judy needed a dentist who specialized in treating disabled patients requiring special care. She needed to be sedated so her mouth could be kept open. Over the years, some teeth had to be pulled and others had parts drilled away. After a visit to the dentist, Judy always came home groggy and with a mouth full of dried blood from work on her gums.

Judy was incontinent and wore diapers. I often changed those diapers, and I remember it made me feel very grown-up. It somehow never bothered me, whether it was a pee or poop diaper. It was just part of what needed to be done, and I was proud that I could help. After all, she was my sister, and I would do anything for her. I think that, because of the experience, I never shied away from cleaning up messes, no matter how gross. In fact, on my very first day student-teaching in a particular kindergarten class in January, a little girl got off the bus with vomit all over her mittens. She wasn't ill, just carsick, so she remained in school. My thoughts went out to her mother who, at the end of the day, would be greeted with a plastic bag carrying her daughter's mittens caked in dry vomit. I helped clean up the little girl and then washed the mittens in the bathroom sink. It was totally unnecessary, of course, but I wanted to be helpful, and the vomit was, just like my sister's dirty diapers, something that needed to be cleaned up, and that was that.

Though she could never tell us, I believe Judy was capable of love, and she clearly had her favorites among family and friends. She always responded with smiles or laughter when anyone in the family interacted with her. Well, sometimes with squeals of disapproval, as when our brother Orin joked with her, but that always ended in laughter as well. Her face lit up when my children came into the house. And when we were younger, the room would reverberate with the sounds of enjoyment while she and I danced together around the room. Of our family friends, Arnold Mittelman was her all-time favorite. He and his wife, Hattie, would occasionally come to visit. When the doorbell rang, Judy would start screeching with laughter, anticipating what would happen next. Never failing to break his routine, Arnold would enter the apartment and say hello to my parents and to anyone else who was in the room—all except Judy. Then he would begin, "Where's Judy? Where is she?"

We would say, "She's right here."

And he would go on, "Where? I don't see her. Where can she be? Ju-udy, oh, Ju-udy, where are you?" Judy would laugh and laugh and laugh. This would go on for several minutes until finally he would find her, and all would be well.

In the beginning, our family tried different therapies in an attempt to help her. I remember a physical therapist coming to our house, exercising Judy's arms and legs up and down and around and around. In my memory, we were probably two years old, possibly younger. A body brace was made to support her body, from her special shoes all the way up her legs, around her hips, up around her ribs and chest, and stopping under her armpits. She didn't complain when she had to wear it; I think she enjoyed being upright. She would stand in what we called her "standing table." Her body would be placed through a small door into an oblong space that opened at the top onto a large table on which her arms would lie. We would put toys on the table, though she couldn't really play with them. Occasionally an arm would move and knock one, forcing it to roll to another spot on the table. We would laugh and try to get her to do it again. The standing table lasted for a number of years until she outgrew it; I remember Judy getting fitted for a new brace as her body grew out of the old one. I loved it when she wore the brace. I would stand next to her and, though I was about a head taller, it made me feel that we were *more the same*. Identical twins are supposed to be *identical*, and I longed for that from the very beginning, to be like the little girls who lived across the street: always dressed the same, impossible to tell them apart. That's how I wanted it to be with Judy and me: playing tricks, fooling those around us. When we were maybe six or so, I was taking a walk one day with my dad and Judy. A boy from the block came by to say hi and walked with us a bit. He asked about Judy, and my father—patient as always—explained, adding that she and I were twins. The boy was disbelieving. My father tried to explain why we looked so different and that, even though she was so much smaller than I, we really were identical twins. My stomach knotted inside until the boy finally seemed to understand, and I was able to breathe easily again. Twins are so special. I only ever wanted to be acknowledged as special too!

Yet even more than I wanted that special *identicalness*, I wanted a sister. As I grew older, I yearned for someone I could talk to and with about growing up and about my dreams, inside thoughts to be shared with someone only a sister could be. As a teenager, I had a short period of that special relationship with my brother David, who was five years older, but then he moved on and away, and I was alone again. Even after I married and had children, I still yearned for that kind of sister—like the one Carrie, my brother Orin's wife, had. Carrie envied the trips my husband and I took with our kids. I envied her for her sister. If at any time in my life I had been granted one wish, it would have been to make Judy "normal."

I remember a conversation I had with my father once. Judy and I must have been about eight or so. I confided in our dad that I wished I could change places with Judy. He got upset with me and asked me not to say that again. Looking back, I guess that was his way of saying that he didn't want to lose me, but he misunderstood my intent. I wasn't that selfless. I didn't want to *be* Judy—in a wheelchair, unable to feed myself or even sit straight, unable to share my thoughts and my dreams. Yes, I wanted Judy to have all the physical and mental abilities she did not possess, but I thought if we could switch places, then I would use what I knew about walking and talking, and I would be able to overcome all my disabilities. Then we would both be *whole*, and we could live out our dreams together.

Judy was my pal growing up, and we spent many hours together. When I first learned to read at age five, I would read to her every day. We had lots of Little Wonder Books, popular with children at the time, and I would read them to her over and over again. It got to the point where I wouldn't even look at the words, just show her the picture and recite the text from memory. I loved to read the books, and Judy loved to listen to them. We also played board games, and on her turn, I would close Judy's hand around the dice as she sat in her chair, and when I let go, the dice would fall to the floor or onto a table, and I would move her piece around the board. We played mah-jongg in a similar fashion. Our mother played in a weekly mah-jongg game, and once every five weeks, the group played at our house. Judy loved having company and watched the women play until it was time for bed. I watched too and thus learned how to play, and every so often, I would set up the bridge table, take out the set, and play with Judy. I would set up our tiles and hop around from her place to mine, playing for both of us. I conferred with her on which hand she should play, though I could never tell if she really understood or just indicated yes to any suggestion I made. As with all the games we played, she showed enjoyment—though it may have been due more to the attention she got than to the actual game.

Yes, Judy was my pal, my partner. I had friends from school and friends from my apartment building with whom I frequently played, but at home, Judy was my companion. We loved to dance together. Sometimes I would face her in her wheelchair, hold on to her hands, and sway her back and forth, turning her chair around under my extended arm, crouching under hers to spin myself around. Other times I would lift her from her bed and dance with her in my arms.

Then we could fly around the room as the music played on the radio. That was the best, though, lightweight that she was, she would soon become too heavy, and I would have to rest.

Our grandparents lived on an upstairs floor in our apartment building, and we saw them every day. Grandpa would walk into our house and, if Judy was in her wheelchair, he'd head straight for her. He would put out his hand and patiently wait while she slowly, painstakingly, lifted hers up as far as it would go to meet his. Grandma was instrumental in caring for Judy. She helped feed her and watched us when our parents went out. One day—I must have been about fourteen—Grandma asked me if I thought it had been a good decision to keep Judy at home. I don't know what was behind this question, but it elicited an unequivocal *yes* from me. How could it be otherwise? At a time when most children with Judy's level of disability were not kept at home, the idea of Judy living in an institution was unbearable for me. My parents evidently felt the same. When my sister-in-law Carrie was writing a paper for her master's degree, she interviewed my parents. Mom and Dad told her that, at the time of our birth, the conditions of most institutions were, to put it mildly, less than desirable. "Judy understands so much of what goes on around her. It would have been unthinkable to institutionalize her." Though I'm sure I didn't fully understand all that caring for Judy entailed for my parents, I was aware of some of the difficulties, and I have always been so grateful that they chose to face those difficulties and keep my sister at home. Judy was a part of me and a part of my family, and I could not envision, nor would I ever want, a life without her. On whom else could I count nose freckles and compare them with my own—something I did fairly frequently when we were young: two identical noses yielding an equal number of dots. Who else would be such an eager listener to the silly stories I told just to make her laugh? In whose laughter would I otherwise rejoice? I know that Grandma loved Judy, but I felt that she also pitied her, and that bothered me. Pity and love did not go together in my mind. I may have wished

Judy were "normal," but I didn't feel pity for her. There was no room. I loved her too much.

Judy continued to need full-time care for her entire life. A couple of years before our father died, when Judy and I were in our mid-twenties, my parents were able to get a home attendant through the Social Security Administration to help with Judy from Monday through Friday. This allowed my mom to get out during the day, but she was always back by four o'clock so that the home attendant could leave. At that time, Mom fed Judy dinner and put her to bed. Eventually the care expanded to include weekends, and then to overnight, so that someone was there to feed and dress Judy and to transfer her from the bed to the chair and back as needed. Two attendants shared the work, one arriving Monday morning and staying until Friday morning, the other one taking the weekend shift. As Mom got into her late eighties, caregiving and supervision of the live-in attendants became increasingly difficult, accompanied by the worsening effects of the CP on Judy's body.

Judy's spine had been slowly deteriorating, and her sitting was becoming more and more lopsided. At one point, maybe when we were in our early twenties, she started needing something that she could rest her head against so it wouldn't flop down. She had already been sitting on a foam cushion fitted for her wheelchair, and by the time we reached our forties, it became more difficult to place Judy in her wheelchair so she could sit as upright as possible. By the time we entered into our fifties, the home attendants were changing frequently, and the ones who came didn't seem to try to get to know either my mother or Judy. Because it was difficult to put Judy in the chair, they did it only when it was time for a meal. Even then, they didn't work at making her at least somewhat comfortable, so she began to spend most of her time on her bed. My mother didn't make an issue of it, perhaps because she didn't like conflict, or perhaps because by denying the existence of a problem, she didn't have to face it. At this point, Mom was well into her eighties, and most of Judy's care had been handed over to the home attendant. Even though she may have thought the aides could do better, she never complained to the agency. I think at that point in her life, she was tired and felt there was no point in complaining because another attendant would be no better. She recognized that maneuvering Judy's body was just more difficult than it used to be.

It was the middle of August 2005—Judy and I were fifty-three and Mom, ninety-one—when the short dialogue that changed everything began. It started with a phone call to one sister from the doctor of the other sister. After living her entire life in her parents' home, it was now time; there could be no further delays. The doctor's message: My sister's health was deteriorating, care in the home was insufficient, and Judy's life expectancy was at risk. Alternative placement—some sort of nursing home—was the only option.

In the days that followed, calls went out for family support. Mom was angry at not being included in the discussion with the doctor; the doctor insisted he would call Adult Protective Services (ADP), and ADP would find a placement for Judy if we didn't do it ourselves. The family attempted a conciliatory plan: home nursing. The doctor refused, based on his belief that Judy was being neglected at home, and reiterated that he would advocate for placement in an appropriate institution. It came down to our choice of nursing home or the ADP's choice. All this led to ultimate acceptance by the family, believing we really had no choice.

This is the account, seen through the eyes of a sister—a twin sister—sentencing her other half to a life in the care of strangers, for the word "home" in the term "nursing home" is merely a euphemism, with no resemblance to the true meaning of the word. In the nursing home, there is no family. There is no unconditional love. There is no understanding borne of knowing a person one's whole life.

And that's how it was in the nursing home, which I always refer to simply as TNH, where Judy was ultimately placed. Strangers cared for their charges, of whom Judy was only one. I do believe that the aides did their best. There were those who took more time than others, some who talked to Judy as they bathed or dressed her—in particular, one special one who gently rubbed Judy's arms and legs with body cream to combat her dry skin and another who took Judy for walks on days when I couldn't visit. For Judy, I am certain, it would not have been where she wanted to spend the rest of her days. My mother and I would have completely agreed with that. Yet so it was, and we watched the same slow deterioration that the doctor had ironically predicted would occur should we have been allowed to keep Judy at home. But Judy was not at home. Instead, we watched the decline occur in a strange place, in the care of strangers, surrounded by other disabled strangers. So it was.

1

Growing Up and Onward

Before there was even any thought of a nursing home, Judy and I shared many happy years together at home. Her disability may have kept us from some activities, but we certainly had enough to enjoy. Almost every summer until we moved from our apartment in the Bronx to one in Queens when we were fourteen, my family rented a bungalow in the Catskills. There we could be outdoors and, most enjoyably, swimming in the pool. It was a big pool, crowded with the people staying at the bungalow colony. Judy loved being in the water, and I loved playing with her. She would wear her little waist-tube (that's how they kept you afloat in those days) as my mother held her, and I swam nearby. I would swim up to her to say hi, and inadvertently splash water on her. She would make such a funny face! She'd close her eyes and pull back her head, her lips puckered, trying her best to hide from the spray but also enjoying my presence. "Come swim with me," I might say, and I would hold her from behind, and we would swim around together. "Okay, move your arms like this—one arm first, now the other one," I would instruct, attempting to move her arms up and down in the water. "Look, you're swimming!" Or I would face her and hold her on her sides under her arms to keep her from slipping through the tube and pull her around with me: "Whee, here we go!" She would laugh and laugh—a bit like when we danced together in the house, swinging around, light and carefree.

Though we never decorated the house for Halloween, my parents allowed us to go trick-or-treating. Dressed in our costumes, I would wheel Judy down the hallways of our Bronx apartment building with our goody bags in tow. Those who answered the doorbell would drop a candy or two into those bags. I always wondered if they knew that Judy couldn't eat their treats and was secretly happy that it meant double for me. Thanksgiving entailed setting up a long table that ran from the entrance to our apartment down the long hallway, past the large living room, and up to the den. Judy loved having people over and sat quietly in her chair listening to the conversations. On Chanukah, she rejoiced in watching my father, and later my mother, light the candles and in hearing them sing the blessings and the songs that came afterward. Singing was also a highlight of our Passover seders for Judy as she sat, first in my grandparents' apartment, then in my parents' apartment and, still later, in my own house, surrounded by family and friends.

We were thirteen when we took our first plane ride together. We flew to Washington, DC, for a mini-vacation and toured the city. At that time, seeing someone in a wheelchair was unusual, and we were greeted with stares of curiosity from fellow tourists and locals alike. But traveling with Judy had its perks. Of course, there was the preferential boarding onto the plane but also some special treatment on the ground—and I was all about *special*. At the FBI building, for example, on a tour where they demonstrated target practice, after the demonstration, the man in charge went over to the targets, took one down, and brought it back to us. "This is for you," he said, leaning over to speak to Judy. No one else on the tour had received a target. I smiled, a wide, toothy smile, excitement radiating from my eyes, *special* written all over my face. It didn't matter that the target had been given to Judy. I was special by association.

The best part for me on this trip, however, was our visit to President Kennedy's grave. It was 1965, and the wound of his assassination was still relatively fresh. It was a big deal to see the grave with the eternal flame. There was a path leading up to the grave, cordoned off to prevent tourists from coming too close. A uniformed guard approached us, asked if he could take Judy, and undid the chain that kept the public away. The crowd watched as he wheeled my sister, with my family in tow, up the path, right up to that flame. I doubted that Judy grasped the significance of the site or the flame, knowing she had heard that our president had been assassinated but lacked the cognitive ability to understand what that meant. I followed Judy, my head held high, walking straight and tall. My eyes sparkled, my smile seemed to reach from ear to ear, and my heart was beating so fast I thought it would pop right out of my chest. Now *that* was a perk!

The next trip we took involved flying out to California in the summer of 1968. This one included not only my parents, my grandmother, Judy, and me but also my brother Orin and a pregnant Carrie. The highlight of this trip was sleeping in a lean-to in Sequoia National Park—wheelchair and all! No special perks that I can recall, just a glorious road trip—something that others may have taken for granted but that I appreciated all the more because of the tricky logistics involved in traveling with Judy. Thinking about it now, I imagine my parents might have been concerned how Judy would sleep in a strange bed and whether she would fall off during the night, not having the bed rail we had at home. Judy sat relaxed as we set our things up in the lean-to, and she watched quietly as my mother fixed her bed. She started to laugh when I jokingly teased her: "Judy, your bed rail is at home. We're putting your chair here tonight, near your bed. No falling over. No waking us up in the middle of the night. Everyone wants to have a good night's sleep." Whether it was what I said or simple exhaustion from a full day of activity, everyone had a great night's sleep, and we were ready to face another exciting day in the morning.

Judy's next trip was by herself. We were in our early twenties when a friend of the family found a summer camp in Rockland County for the disabled. My parents sent Judy for a month. It was the first time she was ever away from home alone, and the first time since the day she came home from the hospital that my parents were without her.

We were always able to tell if Judy liked something, as she simply did not complain. Complaints from Judy entailed unpleasant-sounding noises, which we referred to as *kvetching*, and mild body writhing. Judy evidently did neither at camp. When my parents called to ask how she was doing, they were told that she was relaxed and either sat quietly or laughed during the activities. She never cried or showed other signs of distress. My mother, on the other hand, ended up in bed for the entire month with a case of sciatica. By the next year, though, my parents were better able to handle the separation, and when Judy returned to the camp the following summer, my parents took a monthlong vacation in Israel. Unfortunately, at the end of that second summer, the camp administrators told Mom and Dad that the care Judy required was beyond their capabilities—her physical limitations simply made her too needy—and although they managed as best they could for the two summers, they would not be able to accept her back in the future. That was hugely disappointing to all of us.

Several additional trips followed, including a visit to our brother David in Minnesota. After flying to Minneapolis, my husband, David, rented a car so we could drive to Wisconsin and see some of the sights there. Staying on the first floor in motels presented no problem. Eating in restaurants was a different story. Along with the dietary restrictions of various family members, any trip to a restaurant always included the other diners' stares at a person with a disability. In addition to the wheelchair, Judy being fed was quite a sight for the novice. The person feeding her would scoop some of the soft or pureed food onto a spoon and slip it into Judy's mouth, much as one would do for a baby. Judy would then use her tongue, inefficient at best, to move the food until it either slid down her throat or slipped out onto her bib, which required the feeder to scoop it up and try again. Unable to adequately control the food in her mouth, her attempt at swallowing would sometimes end in a coughing fit. None of us in the family were new to the situation, of course, and we put up with the stares. The eventful moment of this trip came, however, not in a restaurant but when we drove away from it. In her wheelchair, Judy sat on a cushion placed atop a hard board and leaned her head against a side panel that provided enough support for her to sit upright. A cushioned strap was placed around her middle to ensure that she wouldn't fall out. On this day, when we returned to our car after stopping to eat, we put Judy's wheelchair in the trunk but inadvertently left the seat board on top of the car, only to have it fall off as we drove away. When we reached our next destination, we realized we no longer had it and didn't know quite what to do. It would have been very uncomfortable for Judy, and very hard for her to sit properly without the board. David had the idea of finding a home improvement store, and, sure enough, they were able to cut and sand a piece of wood to the size we needed. We were soon on our way again, with another story to tell to bring laughter to Judy's lips.

Judy made two more great trips with my parents, both to Israel and both for six-month durations. The first, when we were eighteen, included our grandmother, and the four of them rented a house in Jerusalem. My father's sister and her husband lived nearby at the time, and Judy visited regularly with my parents. I stayed home, completing my first year of college, and arrived in Israel to stay on a kibbutz about three months before they left. I visited them as often as I could and walked with them around the neighborhood when my dad took Judy for her daily walk. During the second stay, when we were turning twenty-six, my grandmother was no longer alive, and Judy and my parents rented a house in Haifa. This time my mother hired a young woman to help with Judy. Orin, Carrie, and their two kids, Adam and Jason, were nearby on a yearlong sabbatical, and Judy loved seeing them there. Even in hilly Haifa, long walks in the area were part of the daily routine, something Judy always enjoyed.

At the time of the second trip, my father, at sixty-seven, had been forced into retirement from NYU where he had been a professor of psychology for many years. He was not ready to retire and arranged to teach a class at Haifa University. It was during this trip that my father suffered a heart attack. My husband David and I were due to arrive in Israel for a two-week stay shortly afterward but were not there at the time, so I wasn't able to observe Judy's reaction. I imagine that my mother, calm and collected, kept Judy's routine steady and explained, "Daddy has to go into the hospital, but he'll be home in a few days." Judy may have pouted or even cried when she learned about her father being hospitalized, but she was surely calmed by Mom's positive outlook. She was definitely full of smiles and laughter upon seeing David and me a couple of days later. Dad was released from the hospital shortly afterward and was told to take it easy for a while.

Fortunately, my parents had found Jane, the young woman my mother had hired to help with Judy. She was from England but lived in Israel to be near her boyfriend. In search of a temporary job, she heard that my parents were looking for someone to help with their disabled daughter. Jane applied for the position, and it was immediately clear that she would be perfect. She helped my parents in any way that she could and took Judy for long walks around the neighborhood, talking to her as they walked. "Where should we walk today? Let's see, we went down that block yesterday, so let's give this one a try today. What do you think?"

Judy would answer yes to anywhere Jane wanted to walk. Jane remained in contact with my mother long after my parents returned home and she returned to England (together with her future husband), her letters always causing Judy's face to light up in a huge smile.

Before my parents left for Haifa, Orin, already there, made an audiotape outlining the adventures they were having and sent it to Judy. Judy loved listening to tapes (this was before CDs). While she had a collection of music tapes to which she would often listen, her favorite tape was definitely the one my brother made, full of stories detailing what the family had done up until then. She would recognize his voice immediately and break out in a huge smile, her whole body seeming to wake up in excitement. How she would laugh at his stories, knowing by heart what he was about to say, as she had listened to it so many times at home. That tape kept her happy for months—perhaps even years—until, finally, it just stopped working.

Not long after their return home from Haifa, my parents were able to get a home health aide for Judy. I don't remember the impetus for this—perhaps it was because of my father's heart attack, perhaps because my parents finally learned it was an option. I'm not sure. I only remember it was right at the time of the birth of my first child, Ronen, in 1978. The health-care aide, Cynthia, came first, working daytime Monday through Friday. She was only with us for a month, so I'm surprised I still remember her name. Perhaps it is because this was such a change for us, having someone outside the family care for Judy, that I have not forgotten her. We liked her, and I don't recall why she left, but then the gift of Eulia arrived, and she fit into our family like a glove.

Eulia was vibrant, always smiling and upbeat. She was a take-charge kind of person who needed little instruction on how to care for Judy. She simply let her instincts take over. She spoke to Judy just like the rest of the family did—as if talking to a child but knowing that the child understands what you are saying and is capable of respond ing. When dressing her, she would say, "Which shirt do you want to wear—the pink or blue one? Blue? Okay, relax your arm so I can get it in. You'll look very silly if you go around with one arm in and one arm out." When feeding her: "Open your mouth. Okay, now keep the food in. There you go. Very good!" And when taking one of their many walks around the neighborhood: "It's such a nice day today, isn't it? Why are you making that face? It's not so windy. It's good to be out in the fresh air. Let's see if we meet anyone we know. When we go home, it will be time for your milk. Then I'll put you on your bed, and you can rest and listen to your music." She cared for Judy for ten years.

Judy's love for Eulia was apparent in the way she laughed and in how comfortable she was under Eulia's care. Eulia was there at the time of Dad's death at age sixty-nine and through the birth of my three children, often watching one while I went to collect another from nursery school. She was, without a doubt, a part of our family. In fact, when my second son, Ilan, was about five years old, he and I got into a conversation about what happens when people get older and where they live. He made a remark about always remaining in our house, even when he was old. "When people get older, they move out of their house and move to a new house," I explained. "So I'll go live with Grandma," he countered. I'm not sure what I was thinking when I responded, "Grandma won't be here anymore. When people get really old, they die and don't live with us anymore. Like Saba [his grandfather]." Ilan thought for a moment and then said confidently, "Well, then, I'll live with Eulia!" It was a sad day when Eulia left us to retire in Florida. At some point during her tenure, Eulia started staying weeknights as well as days, and, when my mother began needing help on weekends, Beulah came. Second-best only to Eulia, Beulah took Eulia's place during the week when Eulia left, and Hazel came for weekends. After Beulah's retirement, Viola joined us, then Lanette. They were all good people who cared about Judy, and they worked hard, but there was never anyone else who could match Eulia.

Then, after many years of good home health care, it seemed to fall apart. The attendants who came stayed for only a few days, and they didn't understand that Judy enjoyed having them talk with her, so they didn't bother. They came to do their job and did it minimally. My husband, David, and I began noticing a decline in Judy's interest in her surroundings and in her overall physical condition. As she spent more time on her bed listening to music (the new aides didn't seem to understand how to seat her properly in her chair), she was often by herself. The aides, unlike the previous attendants who had interacted with my mother and talked to Judy, stayed in their room and came out only to attend to Judy or to eat. They no longer took Judy for walks around the neighborhood, and generally sat her in her wheelchair only for meals. As I think back on it, she did seem to be languishing, though I didn't admit it to myself at the time.

Even before this reduced level of home health care, David started thinking of the future and encouraged me to begin looking for a place where Judy could eventually live when my mother could no longer care for her at home, even with the help of attendants. I made some phone calls. As Judy was a Queens resident, I began with United Cerebral Palsy (UCP) Queens. The sad news was that they had nothing to offer us. They had no residential programs and no day programs for someone as severely disabled as Judy. They could not even offer suggestions as to where I might turn for help. I hung up, filled with frustration and disbelief. *This is UCP! Their whole purpose is to help people with CP! What do they mean, they have* nothing *to offer my sister?* To this day, I don't understand it.

Not to be deterred, I contacted UCP of Nassau County and had a very different experience. The wonderful social worker I spoke to explained that, because I was a resident of Nassau County, they would allow Judy to enter into their system. First, she would have to become "known" to them. This meant that she would have to change her doctor from the one she visited once a year in Manhattan to one she would see at the UCP center in Roosevelt, Long Island. That was how we began with Dr. M. The social worker also gave me the name of a couple of residences on Long Island for people with cerebral palsy. When my mom and I visited the first one, it was clear that it was not suitable for Judy, though I couldn't help wishing it were. It was a group home in which the residents mostly took care of themselves with support from live-in caregivers. We looked into the second place, a UCP-owned home on Long Island that was in the process of converting from a nursing home catering to the elderly to a residence/nursing home for people with CP. I set up an appointment.

David, Mom, and I went to take a look. I still remember Marty, a pleasant man in his early forties, who was the facility director. He made an enormously good impression on me, answering all of our questions.

Mom: "What kind of residents do you have here?"

David: "Will someone with Judy's severe level of disability fit in?"

Me: "What do you have to offer Judy?"

Marty responded, "The facility was originally set up as a nursing home for geriatric patients. United Cerebral Palsy bought it and is in the process of converting it to one for CP residents with disabilities requiring more care than a group home, set up for more independent living, can provide. We have residents with varying levels of disability—some with very limited verbal ability, some ambulatory, many in wheelchairs. Judy would not be the only resident requiring total care."

He continued, "Some of our residents attend programs at the local UCP center. For those unable to attend, we have an in-house recreational program where residents can go to hear music, watch movies, or play games. Judy would not be eligible for the UCP center programs, but she could definitely take advantage of the in-house activities."

Marty then took us on a tour. I walked around in somewhat of a daze, trying to take it all in and trying to be positive in my expectation that this would be a good place for Judy. There were residents who were clearly more able than Judy, some walking, many talking to each other. Then a young woman on a bed was wheeled past us. I asked about her, and Marty explained that she was unable to sit in a wheel-chair so was wheeled around on the bed, but that she was nonetheless able to join in activities. *At least,* I thought, *there is someone in this world who is more disabled than Judy* (though I really didn't know that was true, as I couldn't see the true extent of her disability), so Judy would indeed have a place here.

Marty went on to say that there weren't any openings at the present time, but, as the elderly patients were just that—elderly—more spots would open up as time went on. This was fine with us because none of us were ready to place Judy anyway. When we did get a call less than a year later informing us of an opening, Mom was emphatic about not being ready. I did not disagree. David, though less sure about the idea of waiting, didn't argue. The recruiter told Mom to let him know when she was ready for Judy to be placed and he would put her name back on the list. Although I worried that Mom would *never* be ready, I knew that neither would I, and I was perfectly willing to wait a good number of years. It was about seventeen years later, after several years of further spinal deterioration for Judy and less ability for my mother to oversee the increasingly more inattentive home attendants, that the call came from the doctor, and we could wait no longer.

I was at work when Dr. M called. The gist of the conversation follows.

Dr. M: "On Judy's last visit, I noticed that she had lost weight, which puts her significantly below the sixty pounds she has maintained. I don't believe she's receiving adequate care at home. Your mother is aging and no longer able to provide proper supervision to the home health attendants."

Me: [*silence, waiting*]

Dr. M: "It is not safe for Judy to remain at home. For her well-being, it's time for her to be placed in a home that would be better equipped to handle her needs."

Me: [*shock, horror, thoughts of,* How can this be happening? *running through my mind.* I am not ready for this. My mother is not ready for this. What are we going to do?] "I will speak to my mother about what you said."

Over the next few days, I also spoke to my brothers. They were happy to entrust the decision to Mom and me. Though I would have liked them to take a more direct role, I was happy that they weren't putting up any objections. As had been the case years earlier, neither my mother nor I was ready for this move. David thought that placing Judy in a home now would have the advantage of my mother being able to visit her there, thus making the transition easier for her. I wasn't convinced and tried my best to come up with alternatives to placement. My subsequent conversations with the doctor were more in line with begging.

"But what if David and I went more often to check up on Judy? Then we could keep her at home."

"But Judy is more comfortable at home. Maybe we can get a better home health attendant?"

"But how will she manage at a place she doesn't know? How will she be able to communicate with anyone?"

"What if we hired someone on our own to care for Judy?"

And so on.

I tried every argument I could think of, but the response was the same: "If you don't place Judy in a home, I will have no choice but to call Adult Protective Services. If you don't start the process within the next week, I will be making the call." He was firm and unrelenting. All I could feel was my body stiffening in horror at the thought of Judy being placed in whatever low-level state-run institution to which APS might send her.

I called TNH, the home we had visited years before. They had openings. I told my mother, told my husband, told my brothers. Then I told Judy, "Remember when David and I moved from Queens to Plainview? And when [my children] Ronen and then Ilan and then Ari moved from Plainview to live in their own houses? Remember how I told you that when people get old enough, they move away and live somewhere else, but they can visit each other? Well, now it's your turn to move away. Now it's your turn to live in a different house, and everyone can come visit you." She pouted. I thought she would cry. *I was making her cry!* "David and I and Mommy will come visit you in your new house. Orin and Carrie will visit too. Maybe [brother] David and Reida can come visit from Minnesota." She continued to pout, on the verge of an all-out cry. "There will be other people there just like you, who need help doing things. And there will be people there to feed you and dress you. And there will be things to do there. It will be fun." She did not look convinced. There was no smile on her face. I was just thankful that at least she wasn't crying.

The day came for the move. Mom, still unclear about why Judy had to go and not in full agreement about the plan, had packed Judy's clothing and extras, all dutifully labeled with her name sewn or written inside. Everything was ready—every*thing* but not every*one*. We were so lost within our emotions, we forgot to tell the agency that Judy was no longer going to need help at home, so the home health attendant showed up for her Monday morning assignment. Embarrassed that, because of our omission, she had taken the bus all the way from her home and now had to return, we explained what was going on and that we would no longer need her services. She stayed with us while we waited apprehensively for the van. Carrie also arrived to join us, wanting to be there as extra support for my mother and me. So there we all were, a literal bundle of nerves.

Waiting, Judy was quiet but unsmiling. She kept looking at each of us questioningly. She didn't really understand what was happening. I reminded her that she was going to live in a new place. "Remember when you went to camp? Remember how much fun you had?" She laughed at the memory. "'This is like camp," I went on. "There will be lots of people and lots of things to do. And now you'll be just like me and David, and like Ronen and Ilan and Ari, and leave your house and go to live somewhere else." I'm not sure who I was trying harder to convince—Judy or myself.

The drive to TNH is somewhat of a blur. I was so caught up in the trauma of the move, I can't even remember how my mother got there. I took my own car because David had to work. Did my mother come with me? Did she ride with Judy in the van? I have a vague recollection of the van driver saying that she could not ride with them and of my worrying about Judy being alone. A vague recollection of assuring Judy, "Okay, you're going to go in the van, and we're going in the car, and we'll meet you there very soon." I do remember Carrie driving her own car, following me all the way. I took the slightly longer route (What was I thinking? Did I not want to get there before Judy?) that allowed me to cross over water two extra times. Seeing the water always brought me a level of comfort, and I definitely needed comfort on this day.

Carrie later asked, "Why were you driving so slowly in the right lane? I was so nervous, continuously having to slow down to allow for cars entering the parkway!" She must have had her own apprehensions related to the day! I thought, *Oh gosh, I caused more distress! I thought driving more slowly would help her overcome her nervousness about driving alone on an unfamiliar road. Instead, it just increased it.* One more trauma added to the day.

We arrived at the home after Judy and were told her room number and that we'd find her there. She was on the third floor, sitting in her wheelchair in her new "home." Her roommate was not in the room at the time. I was happy to see that Judy's bed was by the window—a little bit away from the hallway and the overwhelming unintelligible sounds of residents and foul smells of dirty diapers. I was trying so hard to feel positive, to convince myself that this was for the best and that Judy would acclimate and begin to enjoy her new surroundings. So many emotions rumbled around inside me. So much that I tried to absorb. As they completed Judy's check-in, they asked if we wanted to sign a DNR in case of emergency. I tried to explain to my mother why she had to sign. Confused, or more likely bewildered by what had transpired and unable to understand how and why any of this was happening, she signed. I heaved a sigh of relief. At least if something terrible happened, I wouldn't have to worry that Judy would be resuscitated and possibly spend the rest of her life in a vegetative state. We stayed with Judy for a while, and then it was time to go home.

Exhausted beyond belief, Mom and I returned to my house. We didn't talk much through dinner, and Mom went right to bed. When he returned from work, I gave David an overview of the day. I then turned on my computer to let my friends know how it all went, and before the day could come to an end, I sat down to write . . .

Journal Entry
August 29, 2005
Moving Day
I'm too tired to think, but I want to share today. In short, it sucked. It's horrible. My first thought is to say it's a terrible place, but that's not really true. The staff are very nice and seemed concerned. It's what they call the "residents" that make it so bad. They're all so disabled! Many of them are young, much younger than Judy and me. It's just so sad. They sit around and don't do much of anything. Most of the ones who speak can barely be understood. And the worst part, of course, is that Judy is just like them, even worse. So I walked around on the verge of tears all day, wishing I never had to go back. I left my sister there, and I expect

she's crying right now as I write this. She has probably been crying on and off for three hours. Mom (who is staying at my house for now) and I left her at 5:30, and someone was about to begin feeding her dinner. She may have been okay for that, but most likely not afterward, and no one there would know what to do. Even if they did, it probably wouldn't help. Judy doesn't know them, and they don't know her. How can she feel comforted by strangers?

Way back when I first found this home, I remember Marty, the director, telling me that their policy was that when they take in a new resident, the family isn't allowed to visit for a month. I was horrified at the thought. They've since changed ownership—the home is now privately owned—and they no longer have that policy. For that change in policy, I am grateful—despite how difficult it is for me now.

It was pretty terrible saying goodbye to Judy today, and I'm holding myself back from calling the place because I couldn't bear to hear that she's been crying. Instead, I'll just go back tomorrow and go through the whole separation all over again. I'm imagining that tomorrow will be worse because now Judy knows that we'll be leaving again, and that she'll be all alone. How did this ever happen?

I ache for my mother because she has nobody to cry to, and I know she doesn't want to cry to me. When days go by and things get better (I pray), don't ever let me tell anyone that this wasn't so bad. It wouldn't be true.

2
TNH: A New Life for Us All

The next day, the day after that dreadful one when Judy was left in the care of strangers in a home that wasn't hers, Mom and I began organizing Judy's new room. We started our day shopping for a table for Judy's TV. Judy spent a lot of her time watching TV at home, so we thought she would find comfort in being able to watch in her *new* home. *If she can watch her favorite TV shows, maybe she'll start to feel more relaxed. Maybe it will help her adjust.*

"Debbie, we can bring the TV she has now, but we need something to put it on," my mother said. "Let's go look for something to put the TV on, and we'll take it and the TV with us when we visit Judy later."

After visiting multiple stores and discovering that I was not made for the slow-paced walking of a ninety-one-year-old, we failed to find a suitable table for a reasonable price. "Mom, what if we just take one of those wooden snack tables I have at my house and put the TV on it? Do you think it will be able to hold the weight?"

Mom agreed, saying, "Yes, I think that would be fine, and Judy won't care. She's not fussy about that kind of thing. What's important is that she keep some of her routines. The snack table will certainly do for now. We can always get something else another day." Sometimes *simple* turns out to be the best answer to a problem.

We drove to Judy after lunch. She started crying when she saw us, and I wondered if she was just relieved that we had come back and hadn't simply abandoned her there. I tried to pretend everything was normal. "Hi, Jude! Look at you in your new room! We brought you your TV and a table to put it on. Now you can watch your shows." She stopped crying, but she didn't smile. Her face was expressionless, and she appeared unconvinced that the TV would make a difference in how she was feeling.

While we were there, the physical therapist came in to assess Judy. I was happy because we hadn't set up an appointment, and Mom and I were interested in hearing what she had to say. "It appears that physical therapy will not benefit Judy at this point, but I will suggest that someone come into the room on a daily basis to stretch her arms and legs." The PT's assessment took me back to my early childhood when a therapist had come to the house to move Judy's legs up and down, bending them at the knee and stretching them out again. The therapist at the time didn't think that even that little bit of physical therapy was helping in any way, and it soon stopped. Looking back as an adult, I wish my parents had fought harder for the service. I think that, though it would not have led to Judy walking, it might have kept her muscles more limber. At TNH, as much as I wished Judy could benefit from actual therapy, I thought, *Well, bending and stretching is better than nothing—and certainly more than what she was getting at home.*

After the PT evaluation, the recreation director came in and asked a lot of questions about what kinds of activities Judy liked. That seemed like a real positive to me, but Judy just sat, unsmiling, her head down, showing no interest.

The speech pathologist arrived next. All these evaluations were evidently part of the intake process for new residents. To be honest, they may have mentioned that various personnel would be coming in to assess Judy. Still in a state of disbelief that Judy was now going to be living in a nursing home, I hadn't been able to process all that I was told, so I was very glad that Mom and I were there when all this was happening.

When I heard about the speech evaluation, I hoped it meant Judy would be able to learn an alternate form of communication. Years earlier, a speech pathologist friend of mine had suggested that we take Judy for therapy at the Queens College Speech and Hearing Department. My mother took her to several sessions over a period of five months. They tried teaching Judy to use her eyes to look at the right armrest of her wheelchair for a given "choice one" and her left armrest for "choice two." Judy didn't seem to be getting the hang of it, and it was hard for my mother to get her there, having no means of transportation other than calling a taxi, taking Judy out of her wheelchair, loading the heavy chair into the trunk, taking it out again upon arrival, and seating Judy back inside. The therapist felt that progress, if any, would be too slow and too far into the future to make continuing worthwhile. At the time, I thought, *I'm disappointed. I was really hoping that this would work. Maybe it hasn't been long enough, even though she's not looking at all at the pictures on her chair. It seems like she's incapable of holding her head in such a way as to focus on the chair arms.* Mom agreed, and said, "Even the therapist doesn't think it's helping, and it's so hard to get Judy in and out of the cab with only the cab driver to help me." We agreed to discontinue the therapy.

Now, at TNH, I thought we could try again, and maybe they could find something that would work. But as it turned out, the therapist was coming in only to assess Judy's swallowing to determine what kinds of liquids she should be getting. "Plain juice is too thin. It either spills right out of her mouth or goes down the wrong tube and causes her to cough. She needs something thicker. I'll tell the staff to switch the plain juice to nectar," was all she had to offer. She wanted Judy to go for a more complete assessment at a radiologist's office. I kept quiet but disappointedly thought, *Oh. No communication help. Just drinking.* And I worried, *Ugh. How's a visit to a radiologist going to go? They're going to take Judy to another new place with another new doctor who doesn't know how to treat her? I don't know if that's going to go over well with her. Am I going to be able to go with her when the time comes?* I needn't have worried. It never happened. Lots of things that were supposed to happen never did. It was easier to let them go, not worry about all the what-ifs over which I frequently agonized, and instead give in to what those in charge were doing and saying. It was easier to stay quietly in the background, even though I also knew that sometimes we have to break out of what's easy and step up—speak up for those who can't and advocate for those who have no other voice. Looking back, I wish someone would have pushed me to do that for my sister, because I should have, could have fought for her to receive those things that would have made her life better. Even if nothing changes in the end, going to battle for a loved one at least provides the satisfaction of knowing that you tried.

A little while later, my mother and I took Judy up to the fourth floor to a large rec room where they were playing bingo. Judy looked around and promptly started crying. When Judy cried, she could be quite loud. It might start small, but it often ended up as a full-blown wail. We had to leave. When we got back to her room and mentioned to an aide that bingo didn't work out well, we were told that earlier in the day, Judy had been taken to listen to a singer who sang oldies and, though Judy didn't smile, she didn't cry either. *Bingo is new for her. Maybe if they were playing mah-jongg, she might have liked that. She does like music, and she's more likely to enjoy watching a person performing than a bunch of people sitting in front of a table playing a game she doesn't know. I wish they had singers here all the time. I hope that when singers do come, they'll sing songs that Judy likes. I wish I could control what kind of entertainment they have. I wish I could control the entire situation!* I wish, I wish, I wish . . . How often it is that we wish we had control over situations that are impossible to control. How frustrating it can be. So much time and energy wasted wishing for the impossible. How much calmer we might be if we just let go of those things over which we are powerless.

We didn't spend as much time with Judy as we had the day before. To be honest, I wanted to leave after about an hour and a half. But I didn't think Judy would be okay with that, so we stayed until her aide came in to feed her dinner. I thought that would be a good time for us to go because Judy liked to eat, and it was an activity that might keep her mind off our going. My mother said Judy started to cry as we left, but I thought I saw her opening her mouth for a spoonful of food, and I didn't hear her crying as we walked down the hall and waited for the elevator. I took that as a good sign.

The following morning, however, was not a good one. I woke up feeling unrested and unsettled, as if something were out of place. My stomach was tied in knots. David did his best to cheer me up with his optimistic confidence: "Everything will be okay. Judy will have things to do. There are activities she'll enjoy. We'll take her for walks. She loves walks. There are people there like her. Most importantly, she'll have people taking care of her, not like the home health attendants she had at your mother's house who hardly did anything."

I felt a little better but still was not convinced. I just kept asking myself, *Did we do the right thing? Did I do the right thing?* I felt the choice had been mine. My mother certainly wouldn't have done it, and my brothers just went along with my decision. Yes, the doctor had threatened us with Adult Protective Services, but maybe we could have fought it. And maybe we should have. Yes, I agreed that she wasn't being cared for particularly well at home because my mother just wasn't able to be on top of it anymore. But I wasn't convinced that her care was really going to be so much better at TNH to make it worth what we were all going through. So what if Judy's quality of life wasn't so good at home? Was it really any better at TNH, where she was always worried and afraid and where people cared for her on a superficial level and the people who looked after her also looked after twenty others? *Honestly*, I thought, *would it be so terrible if Judy didn't live longer than the two years that her doctor predicted if she'd remained at home? So, being in TNH may prolong Judy's life. What's so great about that?*

I felt all along that this was the worst choice for my mother, but I had convinced myself that it was good for Judy and good for me. On that morning, though, I wasn't at all certain that it was such a good choice for Judy. True, everyone said that Judy's transition would be easier if my mother were alive to visit her, but I started to wonder. *If Mom passed away before Judy went into a home, it would be traumatic for Judy, but is it really any less traumatic now? Now, even though Mom can visit, a new separation occurs every day, over and over again.*

I used to worry about how I would handle my mother dying and having to place Judy by myself. I thought I needed my mother to be here and help me with Judy's transition into a home. You know what? I had to deal with Judy's placement on my own anyway, and I did it pretty quickly. What I thought would be easier for me—having my mother there with me—turned out to be harder. When Judy was placed, instead of worrying just about her, I had two people I loved to worry about. It turned out to be easier for no one, and I continued to wonder—was it really necessary?

Judy wasn't the only one who had to become accustomed to a new way of life. My mother would be living alone for the first time in her life. Though she thought she would be fine by herself, with no Judy and no home health attendant, I didn't agree. She was, at that point in her life, too forgetful, and I was afraid she'd forget something important, like the fire under the teakettle.

"I think it would be a good idea to find someone who can live in the apartment with you," I suggested.

Mom: "What do I need someone to live with me for?"

Me: "Well, you've always had someone living in the house with you."

Mom: "I don't need anyone to take care of me. I'm fine by myself."

Me: "Well, just someone to be there so you wouldn't be alone."

Mom: "Who would I get to live with me? Anyway, I'm not sure I would want someone else living in my house. And it would have to be someone who understands keeping kosher."

Me: "Well, let's see if we can find someone, and then you can check her out and make sure you like her."

Mom: "You can try, but I don't think it's necessary."

My hope was to find someone whom she would not only like but who could drive and provide Mom with transportation to Judy. Also,

someone to clean and grocery shop when my mother was too tired—
or at least go to the market with her. I didn't hold out much hope that
we'd be able to find someone my mother would accept who could do
all of the above.

The only good I saw come from Judy's placement was that I no
longer had to worry about what would happen to Judy if something
happened to my mother. As David had often said to me, "Judy can't
stay in the house if something happens to your mom. The home
health attendant can't stay with her alone. We can't take care of her
in our home. It's not suitable, with the bedrooms on the second
floor and no place for her—plus the home health attendant—to
sleep. We can't wait for your mother to die." It was a harsh truth
that I didn't like hearing, but he was right. My mother's aging
was becoming more and more of a concern. Filled with despair, I
thought, *Great! So now I have to worry about my mother* and *Judy*
all the time. I spent a great deal of time worrying, as many of us
do when the future is so uncertain. We engage in so much *what-if*
thinking and worrying about possible future occurrences that we
frequently cause ourselves undue stress. If only we would remind
ourselves that we are unable to foresee the future, so there is little
benefit to worrying about it. How much less stress we would have
if we dealt with real events as they occurred. Yet, worried or not,
I was determined to not go back on the decision. For one thing, I
could never go through the placement process again. For another, I
don't know what I could have done differently. I do think, though,
that the experience changed me. I think it changed my mother, and
it changed Judy too. I think we were all sadder for it.

On this third day of Judy's stay at TNH, David, who had been tied up
with some important business guests, paid his first visit. Talk about
two different views of the same scene! I walked into a strange building, saw strangers all around me, and rode the elevator to the third
floor where I was accosted by the smell of urine and feces as I stepped

out. I saw the daunting presence of disabled people, many idling in wheelchairs in the hallway outside their room, some ambling about up and down the hallway.

David's eyes saw a whole different scene. He walked into a building filled with people not unlike Judy and caregivers who would provide what she needed. His eyes saw a place that was going to take care of his sister-in-law. Where I saw a sad, displaced Judy sitting in a room that wasn't hers, with a roommate she didn't know and couldn't talk to, he saw the hope of a better future. "What a great place. So many people like Judy. She looks very good. She's getting adjusted. Look what a nice room she has, with her bed right next to the window, and she has a roommate, so she won't be alone." *Does he really believe this, or is he just trying to convince my mother and me, and maybe himself, that we did the right thing?* I wondered.

When we got into bed that night, I reiterated my concerns about Judy's placement, and David repeated his encouraging and sensible remarks. "It will be okay. Judy will adjust. Your Mom will adjust. It's better for everyone this way. It would be too hard if your mom died and then Judy got placed. She can't stay at home when your mom isn't there to take care of her. You know I'm right. It's inevitable that Judy go into a home, and now is the best time to do it." I wanted so much to believe what he was telling me. With that on my mind, I got up to do some writing. Writing always helped me relax.

Journal Entry
August 31, 2005

I'm trying to decide whether the second day was better or worse than the first. I was just as nervous that Judy would be upset when we left, just as worried that the aides wouldn't know what to do if she cried, just as ready to weep at the drop of a hat, and just as exhausted. The better part, for me at least, was that the place seemed less depressing than it had originally—maybe because seeing the people wasn't a shock. The worse part was that Judy started crying when we arrived and cried—loudly,

I might add—two more times while we were there. That was hard, and once, my mother started crying with her.

I'm not sure if my mother was able to hear when the nurse told me that Judy had cried a lot before we got there, and they couldn't get her to stop. For once, I was glad for her hearing loss. Judy was dozing while we were there. I didn't know if it was exhaustion from crying or just giving up. She looked so thin and frail. The nurse supervisor said she had ordered a chest X-ray for Judy because she'd heard something in her breathing. They were going to come to the room, but no one came while we were there.

We only stayed for two hours today. My mother was really tired, and Judy was sleepy as well. I wanted to wait until the aide came back, but we finally decided to leave. So we actually got home early enough to stop at the butcher and have dinner at a normal hour. My mother went to bed at 8:30!

I'm really worried about Judy, but I realize that this was only her third day (even though it feels like her third month). I only got teary once, and I think my mother was the same. That was a positive. Mom still doesn't like it, though, and every now and then asks me to remind her why Judy is there. I don't have an answer.

I have more to say, but I'm so tired—too tired even to think. The whole situation is so draining that I walk around in a kind of fog. As I drove the forty-minute trip home today, I tried hard to concentrate on the road. I kept having to remind myself of where I was, what route I was taking, and where I had to exit. What's really weird, though, is that I feel like everything is strangely déjà vu. The place, and so much of what's been happening, seems very familiar. And yet it's only familiar as it happens. Before it happens, I don't have a clue as to what will come next. Does that make any sense?

Tomorrow we're going to go earlier. It's hard to sit there while Judy is resting in bed. There's only one chair, so one of us ends up standing or sitting on the bed. That's fine, but it's really hard just watching her rest. I'm hoping that, at some point when Mom is back in her own home, she can visit Judy between twelve and two, and I can come after work.

I don't know how long I'll continue visiting daily—that will depend on how I feel Judy is doing. I'm not sure if Mom will be able to visit every day either, so I'm thinking that maybe we can take turns. But we're not up to that yet.

3
Trying to Adjust

September had always been such a happy time for me. After returning home from our summer at the bungalow colony, my mother and I would shop for new school clothing. I always found the idea of starting a new school year to be very exciting, even beyond childhood and into my years as an early childhood educator. How much there was to discover! How many new adventures there would be! Yet here we all were, September 1, day four of what I would never think to call an adventure, all of us exhausted. I decided that Mom needed to take it a little easier, so we held off our visit until noon. In the time before we left, Mom took three naps. I tried focusing on my schedule for work, but I could barely concentrate. Reading a book was completely out of the question.

Judy seemed to be having a better day and appeared surprised to see us when we arrived—maybe because she remembered camp, where she had no visitors, or perhaps because she was in a location other than her room, which is where, up until now, we had found her each day. She was sitting in her chair at the nurses' station when we got there and broke out into a broad smile when we came into her view. She thought it was funny that we found her there after looking for her in her room. "Jude! There you are! We went to your room and there was an empty bed! What's going on around here?" we joked. She laughed loudly. Right away, my mom suggested that we go out for a walk, so we stopped at the nurses' station to get a pass, required for anyone taking a resident out of the building, and went outside.

We walked up the block, but the sun was in Judy's eyes, and she was forced to close them. "Let's turn around and walk the other way so she can see where she's going," Mom said. We about-faced, and when we got back to the front of the building, my mother was ready to go back inside. "Judy, are you ready to go back in?" she asked. Judy grimaced, indicating no, so Mom went inside the building, and Judy and I walked a bit more before going inside ourselves. As we continued our walk, Judy sat relaxed—no twisting her head around like she would do when she wanted to be somewhere else. With her face in the shade, she was able to keep her head up and look around as we walked and talked.

"Isn't it a nice day? No wind in your face today," I said, leaning over her so she could see me. "Let's see what kind of stores they have around here. There's a gas station over there. And I think that one is a little food market." We continued walking, and I pointed out other stores and places we passed along the way, until it was time to return.

When we got back inside, we sat for a few minutes on the patio and then went back up to Judy's room. We didn't know what to do there, though, and she started twisting and vocalizing complaints, indicating that she didn't want to sit there and wanted to do something else. Mom was dozing in the chair, so I took Judy for a walk down the hallway. We passed the new sensory room containing different objects to stimulate the senses. The woman in charge invited us in, and she tried a few things with Judy. She found something that Judy seemed to like. It changed colors as you held it and had soft brushy things that, with help, Judy touched with her hands. After a few minutes, Judy started twisting and making her I-don't-want-to-be-here-anymore noises, so we went across the hall to try out the sing-along. Jennifer, the recreation woman, was singing karaoke to oldies music, and I thought Judy might really like that. We stayed for a few minutes until Judy indicated she'd had enough.

The idea of a rec room brought back a memory of Judy's school. Not a regular school—that was just what we called it. I went to school, and

Judy went to school. Hers was actually a recreation program provided by the New York Philanthropic League that she attended twice a week from about the age of seven. Judy always knew when it was a school day. She would wake up early, relax so that my mom could dress her easily—"Today you can wear your purple shirt to school!" —eat breakfast without a fuss, and leave the house at about eight o'clock. She would ride a wheelchair-accessible bus provided by the center into Manhattan and return home around two—just a part-time program but enough to give her a break from being in the house and provide something different for her to do. This began years before Public Law 94-142, the Education for All Handicapped Children Act, provided free appropriate public education to all children ages three through twenty-one in 1975. It always saddened me that Judy was never able to benefit from the law by getting an actual education and services, though she did attend her recreation program well into her thirties.

At the program, Judy would do arts and crafts, paint pictures, or make clay sculptures. The leader would hold the appropriate tools in Judy's hands and move her hands for her. Judy often came home with remnants of paint on her hands and arms and a painting or other project she had completed, and her face would light up when we got all excited over it. "Wasn't it fun to get your hands all yucky in the paint? Let me see your fingers—yep, I see green over here and some yellow over here . . ." I was told that activities in the rec room at TNH included arts and crafts, and they sometimes held a sing-along. Because Judy had been so happy going to school, and she loved listening to music, I thought the rec program at TNH might bring back happy memories and help her adjust. Unfortunately, though, the activities at TNH all happened during Judy's rest time, so she didn't have many opportunities to enjoy them.

After the visit to the rec room, Judy's head started to droop, and her eyes closed. Rather than have her fall asleep in her chair, I brought her back to her room. The aide opened the wheelchair straps and lifted Judy out of her chair. With one hand behind Judy's back holding her under the armpits and the other hand under Judy's thighs so that she remained in a semi-sitting position, she placed Judy on her side on the bed with a light blanket covering her legs and chest. I set up her tape, and then Mom and I said goodbye. I left feeling good that Judy didn't start crying. The only thing I was worried about was that the music tape I put on would end and no one would turn it, so she would have nothing to listen to if she didn't actually fall asleep. But I tried not to think about it.

That's one thing I realized as I was on my way home that day: *I leave there and go home, and I don't have to think about it. Judy doesn't have that option.* And though Judy was never far from my mind, there were many distractions at home and at work. Aren't we the lucky ones, then—those of us who can come and go as we please, who are able to distract ourselves from thoughts we don't want to deal with at the moment, and who have the power to decide for ourselves the direction of our lives?

Back at home, I continued working on some sort of plan for my mother for when she returned to her apartment, and I was having a hard time. I guess my distress and emotional exhaustion over the past few days led me to get upset, maybe even a little angry, during a phone call with Carrie that night, when I was faced with yet more tasks to deal with, now having to do with my mother. Fortunately, I managed to keep my feelings to myself because Carrie was really trying to be helpful. She had been calling every night to check in. "How did today go?" "How was Judy?" "How was your mom?" "How are you?"

I would fill her in on the day's events. "Judy seemed okay while we were there. We took her for a walk." "My mom is tired, but I think she's getting used to Judy being in the home." "I'm exhausted but hanging in," and so on. On this particular call, Carrie started talking about a companion for my mother.

"A friend of mine has a daughter who is going to school at St. John's. I asked her if she knew of any students who might be interested in living with your mother, and to ask around."

It sounded promising to me. I told Carrie what I had been doing. "I called the Jewish Family Services agency, but they don't have anything like that, though they gave me two numbers to call. One of them will call me back. The other didn't have what we're looking for. I want someone who can drive my mother to TNH, do housecleaning, maybe occasional laundry, shop for or with her, and watch out that the stove isn't left on. Mom, of course, doesn't think any of that is necessary."

"You should call your local synagogue, and maybe the rabbi knows of people who are looking for work like this."

"I doubt it, and anyway, I wouldn't know who to call in Queens."

"You can look it up in a phone book."

"I don't have a Queens book."

"Well, your mother does!"

My shoulders tensed, and my back went up. I didn't answer. I felt that it wasn't going to end well if I did. Instead, I kept my thoughts to myself. *It's okay for me to schlep to Queens to look at my mother's phone book? She could call information if it's such a great idea.*

Then she suggested, "You can also go online and put in (I forget what she suggested exactly to *put in*) to get names of agencies."

"Maybe you can go online and get the information," I asserted.

"I'm really busy right now with school starting next week and all," was her response. I very well knew how much time it takes to get ready. After all, my school year was beginning as well. And that's when I really almost lost it. I did everything I could do not to say anything nasty. I don't think I had ever gotten angry at Carrie before. She's a wonderful, kind, and caring person. I was just so tired, and fatigue can lessen our ability to cope. I think I didn't answer her (or maybe just said, "Uh-huh"). At that point, I just wanted to get off the phone. *So David and I do all the visiting and all the schlepping, and she does the suggesting? I would just like to know who put me in charge here,* I thought. But I had the answer: circumstance. *I live the closest. I'm the daughter. That's the way it happens.* I understood it, but I resented it.

And then I thought, *Where is our brother Orin in all this? It shouldn't be Carrie's responsibility to find someone for my mother or to worry about how Judy or any of us is adjusting. She's the daughter-in-law. Orin is the son and brother. He couldn't come when Judy went into TNH because it was his first day of school. What about my first day at school?* I kept this frustration to myself as well. I was aware that emotional stress can have a negative effect on relationships, leading to quarrels and hurt feelings. I knew the importance of backing down when you feel your anger or frustration rising and remembering that it is the relationship that is most valuable. So, agitated as I was, I began a calming-down technique I knew: Breathe. Deep cleansing breaths. In through your nose, out through your mouth. In through your nose, out through your mouth. One more time. In through your nose, out through your mouth. Feel the tension flow from your body. *Ahh, so much better!*

Though Orin and Carrie weren't providing as much support as I would have liked, both were clearly concerned about Judy's well-being and felt it important that they see her and continue to be a part of her life. They scheduled a visit to Judy for Sunday. It was a good time for them because they were off on Monday, Labor Day, so it would be manageable. I got the feeling that it would be a while until they visited again. And I did understand the distance issue, as they had to travel from southern New Jersey. I suppose it helped ease the resentment a little.

Interestingly, I didn't resent my brother David even though he was mainly staying in the background and wasn't able to visit. Though he's five years older than me, I've always been somewhat protective of him, possibly because I felt he was so vulnerable when it came to Judy. He had a difficult time accepting her. As small children, David and I had a close relationship. When I was about two, I became his playmate when he wasn't playing alone in his room with his toy soldiers or out with his friends. He shared a room with Orin, each having a twin bed on opposite walls of their bedroom. David and I would build a fort out of blankets on each of the beds, and I would jump out of my "fort" and run over to his to visit. He would invite me in, and we would pretend it was his house. There followed years when I became the dreaded younger sister, and our relationship became the older brother teasing the younger sister whenever the opportunity arose. A bit later, when I was eleven or so, and David had taught himself to play guitar, he bought me my first guitar and showed me how to play. Then, before he left home for graduate school in Minnesota, we became close again, and I had someone in whom I could confide. David wasn't able to have any of those experiences with Judy.

David stayed in Minnesota after finishing school, making it his home and eventually marrying Reida. To me, it was far enough away that I was accepting of their not visiting. We've always been geographically closer to Orin, and therefore he's always been a more visible part of our lives. Orin also had a much closer relationship with Judy all along. When Judy almost died shortly after birth, Orin, then almost nine, would pray for her. Throughout her life, he felt it was his role in the family to make Judy laugh.

David's difficulty relating to Judy may have had to do with his being the stereotypical middle child. David had been the baby of the family for five years until he was suddenly displaced, not only by twins but by *special* twins, one of whom was disabled. When I think about how Judy's needs must have left *me* feeling somewhat overlooked, I can only imagine what *he* felt. A young child is not capable of understanding the demands of a newborn, let alone one with special needs. Children need attention, and when that attention is suddenly withdrawn, it is not surprising to find that the child's self-esteem suffers. They may ask themselves, *What did I do wrong? Why did they stop loving me?* How vitally important it is for parents to be aware of this and to make sure that a way can be found to ensure the child continues to receive the attention s/he needs and craves. I would like to think that my parents continued to give David attention, but I also have to acknowledge that it was obviously different.

When children don't receive enough attention, some may act out in order to get it. Others withdraw into themselves. David attempted to get attention by goading Orin into hitting him so he could cry and run to our parents. With Judy, he mostly withdrew and had as little to do with her as possible. "There was one time that I slapped her on the leg," he told me years later. "It was because I wanted to watch something on TV, and she got mad and started crying loudly because I changed the channel from what she was watching. I couldn't watch my show because of her, so I slapped her. I felt bad about that slap."

I don't think anyone ever explained to David that the negative feelings he had about Judy were *normal*. As an adult, I understand how important it is that parents of a disabled child be open with all their children about the situation they face as a family. Open conversation allows the children to ask questions and receive confirmation that they are still important, loved just as much as always. It was unfortunate for my siblings and me that my parents never had those discussions with us. David's lack of understanding left him embarrassed about Judy's condition. He didn't want to be seen with her and didn't want to bring friends to the house. As far as he was concerned, it was best if no one knew that Judy even existed. He refused to go to his eighth-grade graduation for fear that my parents would bring Judy. He was surprised when, at one of the bungalow colonies, he introduced Judy to a new friend and the friend didn't condemn him for having a sister like that. I wonder if his move to Minnesota was, in part, a way for him to escape these emotions. Far away, he no longer had to worry about people judging him based on him having such a disabled sister.

Open conversation with our parents might have prevented all that. I remember a particular exchange with David after we were both married and before either of us had children. He had come for a visit and shared his concern about having a disabled child, asking if I had that concern as well. I said I did, but that I wanted a family badly enough that I knew I would have to take that risk. Though we can't control all that happens in our lives, if we don't take action in the direction we want it to go, we give up, and as a result, we lose out in the end. David went on to have two wonderful sons.

Several years before Judy went into TNH, David was diagnosed with Parkinson's disease. And so, in view of the geographical distance between us and the fact that travel had become more difficult for David, I accepted that he and Reida would take a less active role. Whether right or wrong, I directed my feelings of frustration toward New Jersey. Having calmed down after my conversation with Carrie, I sat down to write.

Journal Entry
September 1, 2005

I guess we are adjusting somewhat. But I also feel that we're not adjusting. No one cried today, so that's a really good thing! But I just can't get used to some of the people there, and I can only hope that Judy can adjust. There's one woman who sounds exactly like Judy when she kvetches. This woman kvetches a lot, and loudly, and we can often hear her from down the hall. She really bothers me, and I think she may bother Judy as well. The rest of the people are better, but let me tell you, this is one strange group! It's like being in an asylum. I know it sounds terrible for me to say that, but it's really like that. Most of the residents on this floor, if not all of them, are mentally challenged—and if there's anyone who isn't, I can't imagine how they live there. I wish I could secretly video the place. I'm sure it's not unique, but it's definitely new to me. If I could only come up with the words to describe it to you. It makes me laugh and cry at the same time.

Strangely, perhaps, every now and then I get a wonderfully calming feeling that a routine is setting in and my life can begin to settle down. The feeling comes quickly and, just as quickly, I realize that no, I'm not even close to getting back to settled. At those moments, I am somewhat in a state of despair—not knowing when, or if, my life will ever become normal again. At those moments I feel like crawling into my bed and sleeping forever. But I don't. Not because I'm a wonderful person. Not because I have the strength of a lion. Not because I'm unselfish and deserving of Jewish sainthood. Simply because the other option would actually be worse. I could become totally immobile, unable to get out of bed in the morning, or I could get up, go through my day, and simply do the best I can. Sometimes it's just about how we choose to deal with an undesirable situation. So I make my choice to continue plowing through, and I tell myself that it has only been a few days (did I already say that it seems more like months?), that it will get better, and that we are all doing remarkably well under the circumstances. I do believe that somewhere down the line I will adjust to this, and it's that belief that allows me to go on. Faith and hope are, indeed, such powerful feelings.

My mother appears to be adjusting much better than I thought she would. Sometimes her poor memory and loss of a sense of time seem like a blessing. She assumes that this has been going on for a while—probably the same number of months that it's been going on for me—and because this is how it's been, it's how it's supposed to be. I worry that Judy may never adjust. She may accept her situation without crying all the time—after all, what choice does she have?—but I don't believe she will ever be happy. Some of us in my family may have had a fantasy that going into a group home, with other people like her, would be such a wonderful experience for Judy, and she would love the activities. Now I see that's all it was—a fantasy. One that we, the ones who put Judy in this place, made up to ease our consciences and allow us to be able to live with ourselves. A coping mechanism, not unlike the one my mother subconsciously used when she started believing that Judy had been in the home for much longer than she actually had. Unable to face what happened, she created a defense against the horror of the placement. Not unlike the fantasies I had as a child when I dreamed of being a superhero, running into burning buildings to save people. If I couldn't save my sister, then I at least could save others, and as a bonus, I would be looked at with awe. A coping mechanism not unlike convincing myself that I would one day adjust.

In addition to my anxieties about my adjustment, I find myself fretting over my brother and sister-in-law's visit. I'm thinking about taking the day off altogether so I won't have to deal with it. I get nervous because Judy doesn't like when her sense of order is disturbed, so I worry if she feels something isn't the way it should be, it may bring on tears. Even though I know she'll be happy to see Carrie and Orin, I'm afraid *they might say something that reminds her of home, and that might upset her.*

I have my own ideas about what we should and shouldn't say to Judy, and I tend to think I know how she'll react. I admit I would like to be able to control every circumstance, and when we are in situations in which I envision Judy getting upset, I become very watchful for her reaction to what others are saying. I observe her face closely, looking for any sign of a pout, a suggestion that she may start to cry, and then I step in with a joke or a remark that will ease her mind and cause her to laugh instead. But it's stressful for me. My whole body is on alert, and my mind starts whirling, thinking about what I can say and how I can avert a crying situation. I envision someone saying something about the home or about Judy being in the home that she takes to mean that she should be missing her real home. I envision her lower lip jutting out and her face scrunching up into a pout, just before she starts to cry. Those what-ifs can really mess with my mind!

If I were a stronger, better person, I could do it all: I could visit every day and be happy about it. I could step aside occasionally and allow others to have their turn. I could accept the situation as it is and be grateful for a place where Judy can go and be safe. But I'm not and I can't and I don't want to have to. I wrote earlier that I sometimes get a fleeting feeling that everything is on its way to getting back to normal. Wishful thinking, I guess, is what it really is. I've lived my whole life wishing for the fantasy that everything (i.e., Judy) would be normal, and with the frustration that it cannot be. Why should things be any different now? It makes me so tired, this feeling of total impotence. And, believe it or not, I really do hate to complain. I don't think I have the right.

4
The Visits Continue

Carrie had said that she and Orin would be coming to see Judy on Sunday, still two days away, so Mom and I continued our practice of daily visits. When we got to TNH, Judy was on her bed. Her aide told us that she had tried keeping her in the chair after lunch, but Judy started crying. That was sort of the good news—that the aide was able to figure out what Judy wanted and did it. Judy gave us a big smile when she saw us. "Should we put you in the chair?" I asked.

Her mouth immediately opened and closed, indicating *yes*. The aide positioned the wheelchair, set the brakes, and lifted Judy off the bed, much the reverse of how she would lay her down, so that Judy's body was in a seated position. To get Judy into her chair, one would have to stand with their feet apart—one foot near the back of the chair and one near the front of the seat. A slight swinging motion then set Judy's rear end toward the back of the seat, and her head lifted up so that her back rested against the back of the chair and her head against the headrest. Proper placement involved standing behind the chair and lifting Judy under her armpits so that her bottom sat more snugly in the seat. Because of the curvature of Judy's spine, no amount of lifting could get her bottom to sit squarely in the seat, and I think this step was often omitted. A thick cushioned strap around Judy's middle would then be fastened in the back, and a lap strap buckled over her thighs. When I put her in the chair, I added the extra step of facing Judy and straightening her hips a bit so that she wasn't putting all her weight on one hip. This step, too, was generally omitted by the aides.

Once Judy was in her chair, I asked if she wanted to go for a walk outside. Another immediate *yes*. Before we left, though, the exercise lady came in to do range-of-motion activities with Judy. She said she would come in to stretch Judy's arms, fingers, and legs every day to help with the stiffness. Even though it lasted for only about six minutes, I was glad for any exercise.

Judy's roommate's mother was in the room when we got back from our walk. After introducing ourselves, she told us that Erika had come to the home when it was owned by UCP and had been at TNH for nineteen years, that she has cerebral palsy, doesn't speak, and uses a communication board. "It has pictures on it, and she is able to touch a picture to show what she wants. So, for example, if she wants something to eat, she touches the picture of that specific food. Or if she wants to sit out in the hall, she touches the picture of the chair. She's able to make her desires known, and she likes it here," her mom told us. "I don't live nearby and can't visit every day, but when I come," she continued, "Erika is always happy to see me and is in a good mood." I wished Judy were able to use a communication board and thought how great it was that Erika had the ability to communicate to some degree with others. Knowing that Judy was not able to make her needs or desires known caused a pang in my heart. Then I thought about how long Erika had been there: *Nineteen years! Wow. I can't imagine Judy being in this place for that long. And I can't envision Judy ever being happy here. She may stop crying so often, but I don't think she will ever be happy—even after nearly two decades. How can anyone be happy if they have no way of communicating?* I thought about Erika's situation. *Erika is forty-five years old. She was twenty-six when she arrived. Judy lived at home for fifty-three years, with people who loved and understood her. At least for that, I am grateful!*

I went home that day so thankful that there hadn't been a bed for Judy when we first looked almost nineteen years ago, and that my mother wasn't ready when we were later told a bed had become available. But how frightening and sad it was to think that Judy could live long enough to now be beginning a nineteen-year (or longer) stay. We all want our loved ones to be just that—loved. And I couldn't imagine anyone loving her in TNH.

The next day, I visited Judy by myself while David spent time with my mother. When I got there, Judy was sitting in her chair in her room, listening to me talking on the audiotape I made for her. She seemed content. She looked at me funny, and I realized that she was probably wondering where Mom was. "Mommy didn't come today. She stayed at my house with David." A pout appeared on Judy's face. "Well, she has to go to the beauty parlor so she can look beautiful." Big laugh. "Let's go for a walk." Judy's mouth opened and closed for a yes. She looked so cute in the baseball cap I brought to keep the sun out of her eyes. I took her over to the nurses' station to get a pass, but the nurse wasn't there at that moment. Erika was sitting nearby, facing down the hallway, so I wheeled Judy over and said hello. I joked that Judy and Erika could talk to each other while we waited for the nurse to come back. Erika started laughing. She laughed just like Judy. Judy started laughing because Erika was laughing, and Erika kept laughing, and they were having this laughing conversation. All the tension left my body, my shoulders relaxed, and I broke out into a smile. *This is the first time Judy has laughed here with someone other than one of our family. If only they were able to have this sort of communication without a third person getting it going.*

The nurse returned, and we got our pass and went for a long walk. Judy sat quietly, looking around as we walked. Walking was much easier without my mother because I could walk at a faster pace and not worry about whether Mom was keeping up or getting tired. I knew this wasn't about what was easier for me, but taking Judy by myself afforded me a chance to relax a bit, and I couldn't help being happy about it.

When Judy and I returned from our walk, an aide was delivering drinks to the residents. When I asked if Judy could have a drink, she happily gave her some regular apple juice. *Didn't anyone tell the aides that Judy needs thickened drinks?* Then, before I went home,

I asked her aide if she would be able to turn Judy's audiotape over when it ended. Her reply was, "I'm sorry, I'll be leaving in a couple of minutes, and I won't see the aide who comes in after me." *Where's the transfer of information here? Are the caregivers getting it? Strategies and techniques found to be successful with Judy don't seem to be shared by those who work with her.* I remembered the UCP doctor's previous directive: "Judy shouldn't be lying on her back." It didn't seem to filter down to the aides, and I had found Judy lying in that position more than once. "Judy should have something between her legs so her knees don't rub together," the rehab woman had told me. I seemed to be the only one following that suggestion. Yet I didn't bring it up to anyone. I didn't want to rock the boat. What I didn't realize then was that it was my *right* to rock the boat if I felt things weren't up to par. I forgot that we are the voices for those who cannot speak for themselves.

Driving home that day, I felt my fatigue setting in, and I struggled to keep awake. My mind drifted to trips my family had taken to the bungalow colony in the Catskills every summer. We did not own a car. Going to the "country" involved hiring a driver who would come in a station wagon with an attached trailer that would hold our summer belongings. The trip would take roughly an hour and a half. Judy liked going places and, as long as we didn't get stuck in traffic, sat quietly in the back seat leaning on Mom and looking out the window. Traffic, on the other hand, caused her to twist her body and vocalize her discontent with grunts and other unhappy noises.

I, too, loved going places, and I didn't find the traffic much of a problem. That's probably because, feeling nauseous in the back seat, I would close my eyes and sleep for most of the trip. The movement of the car always lulled me, gently rocking me from side to side, perhaps reminiscent of the baby carriage rides I received as an infant. These days, the trips home from TNH often threatened to put me to sleep, even when I was the driver, even with my mother as a passenger; the gentle bumping of the car on the road was soothing, and I had to struggle to keep my eyes open. Stress can cause fatigue, and I was certainly frequently stressed. Fortunately, I never succumbed and completed all my trips safely.

My fatigue carried over to mornings at home. There were days when I had a hard time getting up and wished I were able to just stay in bed and sleep. The Sunday when Carrie and Orin were to visit Judy was one of those days. The added stress of worrying about how Judy would react to her visitors made me want to skip the visit altogether. I felt, though, that it was important to Mom and decided that if we spent some time there before my brother arrived, we wouldn't have to stay through his visit. Sometimes we just have to relinquish control and trust that others will be able to handle the situation just fine.

I ended up taking my mother to Judy at our regular time, and my brother got there a while later. Judy was in her chair, ready for a walk when Mom and I arrived. Mom waited in Judy's room and chatted with Erika's mother, and Judy and I took a long walk. I was a little nervous that we had established a routine that she was going to anticipate every day, so I told her that now that my school was starting, our routine would be different, and Mom and I wouldn't be coming at the same time every day. "In fact, sometimes just Mommy will come, sometimes just me, and sometimes David." Knowing Judy and her level of understanding, I was sure she understood my words but not that she realized what they implied. I didn't know if she had the cognitive ability to understand *how* the routine would be changing. Her life was so scheduled that I wasn't sure she could visualize any modifications to it. Anyway, it would be happening, so she'd have to adjust.

As I pushed her in her chair, I was reminded of our walks when we were younger—when we were more carefree and looking to have fun. In those days, I would give the chair a big push, and Judy would roll on ahead of me at a faster pace. Then I would run to catch up, yelling, "Wait for me!" Sometimes I would give the chair a smaller push and then walk up alongside it. "Hey, Jude! Hello there! Where are you going? Can I come along?" Judy would laugh and laugh, fully comprehending that she was incapable of controlling her own wheelchair and finding it so funny that she was gliding along on her own, and I would laugh right along with her. Adulthood brought with it more *adult* behavior, and our walks became more ordinary—and definitely safer!

When we got back to TNH, Judy got kvetchy, twisting her body and making grunting vocalizations—unhappy sounds that anyone paying attention would recognize as dissatisfaction with her situation. Mom asked her if she wanted to go on the bed and she said yes but continued fussing, and I couldn't figure out what she wanted. I thought she might be thinking that we were going to leave. I was surprised that she would kvetch about it because she really hadn't in the past. We asked the nurse to get someone to put her on the bed. I could have done it myself, but they had asked that I call an aide. When the aide came in, Judy continued to kvetch. I asked again if she wanted to go on the bed, and again she said yes. So the aide put her down and as soon as she got there, I realized that she probably wanted a drink because on the previous day when we came back from our walk, they were giving out drinks, and I got her one. Sure enough, that's what she wanted. So we rolled the bed all the way up and gave her a drink in bed. The kvetching stopped, and her body relaxed. "Let's see if we can do this without making a mess. We don't want to have to call the aide back and tell her we flooded the place," I joked, getting a laugh in response. I was glad I was able to figure out what Judy wanted. It was so frustrating when we couldn't figure it out, so frustrating that she couldn't tell us. Family members were much more likely to keep trying and hopefully get it. Knowing that the people at TNH wouldn't spend as much time and effort on it was also frustrating, but there wasn't anything we could do about it.

Soon after, Orin, Carrie, and Carrie's mom, Susan, arrived, and my mom and I left. I was so eager to leave that I almost ran out when they came in. I probably would have if Mom could have kept up. My mind wanted to escape into oblivion, pushing down any anxieties about what *might* happen during my brother's visit and whether Judy would get upset about something. Yet as I left, a calmness spread over me at the knowledge that Mom and I weren't leaving Judy alone.

Later, after Orin and Carrie arrived back home in New Jersey, Orin called and reported that their visit had gone well. I breathed a sigh of relief, somewhat humbled to have thought that I was the only one who knew how to speak to my sister. Moving forward, Mom, David, and I made a visiting plan for the next few days. I kept telling myself that, just as we were all adjusting to this whole new experience of TNH, we would adjust to a new schedule. I couldn't believe that almost one week had passed. It seemed like months. When I realized that it had been such a short time, I was amazed at how well we were all doing, though I thought that Judy was still waiting to come home, and that worried me. Back when she went to camp, she stayed there for a while, but she always came home.

The relatively calm feeling I experienced that day was, unfortunately, short-lived. The following morning, I woke up feeling as if I couldn't do it anymore and agitated over how I was going to be able to visit Judy after a full day of work, concerned about how my mother was going to manage on her own and how she would get to TNH to visit, and upset that Judy wouldn't be able to go on her little walks anymore during the week. I realized I just had to keep going one day at a time and do what I could. I was still conflicted about whether this had been a good decision. At times, I was happy we had done it so I didn't have to think about doing it in the future. Then, at other times, I felt I had condemned my sister to a sad life away from loved ones sooner than necessary. I kept thinking how, according to the doctor's prognosis, I had probably prolonged Judy's life, and I was unconvinced that prolonging one's sadness and loneliness could be considered a gift.

Journal Entry
September 4, 2005

I'm glad I decided it would be better for all of us that I not be there when Orin and Carrie visited. I wouldn't know what was going on, and they would surely be able to handle whatever situation arose. Mom and I saw

Judy, and then Orin, Carrie, and Susan spent some alone time with her, and it worked out fine. Sometimes we just have to let go and have faith.

I'm finding it so strange that I'm spending so much time with my sister. When we were young, I considered her a playmate. We used to play games together and dance and stuff. Then I had my own family, and I feel as if I abandoned her. I did see her weekly when my kids were young. David, the kids, and I would go to my mom's house every Friday night for Shabbat (Sabbath) dinner. Though Judy was usually on her bed when we arrived and throughout our visit, we each went into her room to say hello and interact a bit. When my part-time job expanded to include Friday afternoons, there was no longer time for me to pick up the kids and head to Queens, so the weekly visits ended. Of course, we still visited every now and then, and in the spring and summers, David and I would occasionally drive to Queens on a Sunday to pick up Mom and Judy and take them to a garden or arboretum. Judy still loved the walks, and we all enjoyed being outdoors.

Looking back, though, it somehow doesn't feel like it was enough. The walks in the parks eventually became rare and the visits fewer. Picking her up to put her in and out of the chair and in and out of the car became more difficult, and I was busy with my own life. I closed my eyes to my mom's aging and her reduced ability to oversee the home attendants. I closed my eyes to Judy's deterioration. Now, all of a sudden, I find myself feeling responsible for her. I suppose that since my children have grown, I now have more time for her. It's sad that I once could have reduced her importance in my life; that someone so central to me, so vital a part of who I am, can fall into the background; that I couldn't manage to keep both, my sister and my growing children, in my life at the same time. Yet here I am, back in her life again and she in mine. Isn't it interesting how circular life can be?

One of the things I've been lamenting recently is how, when I was growing up, no one told me how hard life can be. I would like to have been better prepared. I think it goes back to the need for family conversation—the necessity of sharing the difficulties we naturally come across as we navigate the world and the importance of thoughtful discussion *and guidance through which we can give our children tools to face those difficulties. If we shelter our children in a cocoon, trying to keep them safe, we do them an injustice. When they are faced with the challenges that life brings, they are unprepared. I feel that may be what happened to me. Strange, perhaps, that I never saw Judy's disability as one of life's challenges. Perhaps because my parents never spoke about it, I always accepted it as part of our life—it was just the way things were.*

I find that my journal writing helps me. It gives me a way to vent my feelings and release some of my stress. Maybe at some point I won't need it anymore. Maybe I'll be better able to accept the situation as it is and deal with the challenges it presents in a more relaxed way. At the moment, though, I'm not ready. I'm sure there will be ups and downs, days when I have to get it all out and days when it doesn't feel so urgent. I think these ups and downs are somehow necessary to the healing process. At least, I imagine, they are a natural part of it.

5

Mom

Life went on, and so did we. It was time for Mom to go back to her own house. I was looking forward to her return home. Not that she was a difficult guest, and not that I wouldn't have had her longer if she'd wanted—it was just nice to know that I would have my space and time back. However, being the worrier that I was, not having my mother here led to more apprehension on my part. She had been married to my father for over forty years and then had the company of Judy and a home attendant in her house for the ensuing twenty-four years. This would be the first time in her life that she would be on her own. To make things easier for her, and less worrisome for me, we hired Grace, Judy's former home attendant, to spend nights with Mom so someone would be there in case of an emergency. I hoped everything would fall into place and I would be able to relax. Too much worrying can be counterproductive, but it is often a result of caring, when we think about the future and are concerned about how our loved ones will fare. Our lack of control over situations can leave us feeling anxious and stressed, and taking control of what we are able to control can relieve some of that stress. I was trying to stay calm and let the future play itself out, one day at a time.

For the next visit, David took my mom, and I went to work. After the visit, David took Mom home to her own house. She was very happy to be there, acting as if it had been such a long time. When I called her after school, she said she had cleaned up a little and she would do a little at a time. I didn't know exactly what she was cleaning up, but as long as it kept her busy, I was happy. I reminded her that Grace would be coming that night.

"Who's Grace?"

I explained.

"How much am I paying her?"

I explained.

"That's too much—after all, what is she doing? I'll use her for the first week, since we committed, and then I'll decide if I want her after that."

I didn't argue. I figured she'd forget the conversation, as she was becoming more and more forgetful over time. I always felt her forgetfulness was exacerbated by the trauma of Judy being taken from her house. I tried to enjoy coming home after work to an empty house, but I couldn't help thinking about who she was now in contrast with who she had been in the past.

Mom and Dad met when they were barely teenagers. They hung out together in a group of kids their age, several of whom ended up marrying within the group, and most of whom stayed lifelong friends. I never heard my parents argue, and the only time I ever even heard them disagree was about politics when I was around twenty. Dad was a professor of psychology at NYU when Judy and I were born. At home, he was the chief dishwasher. Though we had an electric dishwasher in the Queens apartment, Mom used it only when the family put their foot down after a large dinner gathering. Otherwise, after dinner, it was my father's job. Judy loved to watch him and would sit smiling and laughing as he told stories while he washed.

Mom was also a twin, which somehow made my twinship feel even more special. Hers was a fraternal relationship, and her twin was her brother, Maschel (Milton). They were close and, as adults, always lived within walking distance of each other. They spent holidays together, and there were several special birthday celebrations over the years. Mom had a wonderful relationship with Maschel's wife, Dora, and the two sisters-in-law became travel partners after their spouses passed away.

When I had confidence issues concerning my shyness, Mom would tell me that she was also quiet and introverted as a child. "As I got older," she said, "I gained more confidence and started asserting myself more. I spoke up when I felt I needed to and didn't just sit idly by." She felt sure that the same would happen to me.

Mom had always been a strong woman, fully capable of handling any situation that came her way, as seen through her acceptance of her need to give up her career to stay home and care for her disabled child. She was a college graduate at a time when many women did not continue their education beyond high school, and she worked as a social worker in Morningside Heights in Upper Manhattan. She stopped working when she had her first child, intending to go back once her children began school.

I never heard her complain, lament over what might have been, or ask, *Why me?* She did what she had to do and made it work. Her attitude was always, *Things will work out.* Her house and her life were well organized, and we always followed routines—milk snack at four (her children were required to drink four glasses of milk each day), dinner at six. Always practical minded, she and my dad waited to marry until she graduated from Hunter College, then waited six more years to begin a family. Mom was the one who took care of the finances, paying the bills, balancing the checkbook, and budgeting their expenses. When she joined a Jewish women's organization in her neighborhood, she was the group's treasurer.

Always a walker, Mom would often spend her mornings walking to a department store in the Bronx or, later, Queens. Sometimes she would take the subway into Manhattan and go from store to store there. When my husband, David, whom I had met overseas, first came to this country, she invited him to shop with her. As he hated being idle and had nothing else to do until he started school and got a part-time job, he was happy to join her, and off the two of them would go to Alexander's while I went to my college classes. Shopping was Mom's outlet—an escape from hardships and a way to relax—and she would come home with clothing or home goods, many of which she returned on her next trip.

She loved to knit and made many a sweater and hat for her grand-children over the years. She also loved mah-jongg and played in a weekly game, rotating the venue from one player's house to the next in a continuous pattern. I don't remember when or why that stopped. Perhaps at some point there just weren't enough players. Mom was an avid theater-goer and purchased season tickets every year, attending with my father until his death and then with a family friend until that person passed away. She was also an ardent reader and would fre-quently recommend books to me that I would then read and discuss with her.

Mom always wanted to look her best, and she never left the house without makeup and lipstick. Once a week she would go to what was then called the beauty parlor to get her hair done. Each week she would have her hair washed and set, then sit under the dryer with rollers in her hair until it was ready to be combed out. So it was only because of the imminent departure of David to Israel following the outbreak of the Yom Kippur War that she had run home from the beauty parlor, curlers still in her hair, after David's phone call to her there. She waited frantically for me to get home from Queens College so we could get to the airport before he flew out. That image has remained with me to this day.

A few years after the death of my father, Mom started traveling with a friend. Eulia, Judy's wonderful attendant, stayed with Judy full-time, making it possible for Mom to enjoy a week or two on an orga-nized tour somewhere in the US, Europe, or Asia. Judy loved Eulia and didn't mind Mom being away. During these vacations, Mom par-ticipated in many adventures, including white-water rafting down the Snake River out West and, at the age of eighty-five, riding a donkey down a small mountain somewhere in Europe.

Stubborn and set in her ways, she still took the subway into the city at age ninety to shop or go to the doctor, despite our requests for her to take a cab. Physically, she slowed down a lot as she aged, but she continued to walk and shop for groceries or visit my aunt Dora, who lived in her neighborhood. She became more forgetful toward the end

of her life, and I cringed when people suggested that she was suffering from dementia. I didn't think she deserved such a harsh label. I
wanted her to be my mother, never changing, forever. Yet there she
was, at age ninety-one, forced to comply with a decision not of her
making that only served to increase her fragility. It broke my heart to
see her so confused.

Although Mom only wanted a person to stay with her at night, she
told me and David, several times a day, "No one came, and there's no
one here during the day!" We kept explaining that Grace only came at
night. Despite knowing that my mother's memory and sense of time
were fading, I found myself fighting to keep my voice steady and my
irritation in check when answering, for the umpteenth time, "Grace
was Judy's home attendant. She's going to come here and stay over every
night so you don't have to be alone." David similarly struggled to remain
calm. David and I thought it might be better if Mom came to live with us
and tried multiple times to convince her, but she refused. She felt totally
capable of caring for herself and didn't want to lose her independence.
Because she remembered how she felt when her own mother came to
live with her toward the end of Grandma's life, her answer was always,
"No. It is unnecessary. And I will never do that to you."

Bleary-eyed and desperately needing relief, David and I lumbered
on. On Mom's first day home, I drove from Plainview to Forest Hills to
pick her up for a visit with Judy; then David met us there and took her
home. In addition to forgetting that David was taking her home, she
forgot to bring the lunch I suggested that she make for herself ("That's
a good idea. I'll make a sandwich.") and then got annoyed that she
hadn't eaten and David had, and that I was going back to work! She
was also annoyed that I had spoken to the nurse without including her
in the conversation. I had asked about some nightgowns I had bought
Judy the week before that had been taken to be labeled but had not yet
returned. It wasn't that I didn't include her in the conversation; her
hearing loss simply prevented her from participating. "What were you
talking about with that nurse? Why were you being so secretive?" she
challenged, thinking that I was conspiring behind her back.

Maybe this was a result of feeling that the decision to put Judy in TNH had basically been forced on her, but I remembered that when my grandmother lived with us, she would often think we were whispering about her, a natural consequence, it seems, of hearing loss. We knew it was not my mother's fault, though we suggested many times that she get a hearing aid. Whether it was because she felt it would somehow diminish her appearance, or because she felt it announced to the world a weakness, or because friends of hers had complained about their own, I never knew, but she always refused.

Going to and from TNH seemed to become as much of an issue for Mom as it was for David and me. The drive back and forth was really tiring her out, and she started harping on its location. "Where did you find this place?" "Why didn't we put Judy in a place in Queens?" Our repeated response, that there were no places for Judy in Queens, didn't stop her from repeatedly asking about it. David and I decided that once a week would be enough for her to visit Judy, and we arranged for her to go only on Sundays. I didn't feel bad for Mom because she didn't remember whether she had visited today or yesterday or the day before. I did feel bad for Judy because there would be days when no one came to see her. I made my plan—I would visit several times a week, Mom would visit once, and David would likely visit once or twice—and hoped that Judy would adjust.

Journal Entry
September 8, 2005
Oh, gosh, I'm just exhausted! Balancing work and family can be so difficult, way harder than I had thought it would be. So much rumbling around in my head. The emotional fatigue, for both my mother and me, caused by the entire situation; the physical fatigue, for both of us, caused by the commute back and forth to TNH; and the distress over realizing that daily visits to Judy were no longer possible. I just want to sleep and sleep and sleep, and when I wake up, everything will be back to normal, and all this would have been but a terrible nightmare . . .

6

Pendulum

With my plan set in my mind, David and I took my mother for our next visit. We found Judy lying on her bed taking a nap when we arrived at TNH. When we woke her, she gave a quick yes when asked if she wanted to go for a walk. On our return, we heard there was a guitar player in the rec room. Judy grimaced no when asked if she wanted to go on the bed, so my mother took her upstairs to listen to the music. I guess she liked it because she didn't complain. Afterward, we put her on the bed so she could rest before dinner, and before we left, David asked Judy if she liked TNH. She indicated yes. I almost fell over and thought, *Wow, this is great!* Then I realized that Judy's "liking" TNH was most likely temporary and that she still expected and was waiting to go home. And why wouldn't she? We had led her to believe this would be like camp.

The camp staff had told us Judy liked being in camp. "She rarely complains and laughs often. She is relaxed when we take her swimming and puckers her face but doesn't cry when she gets splashed. She goes to sleep quickly at the end of the day and sleeps through the night, waiting patiently in the morning for the counselor to get her dressed and out of bed." After returning home following each of the two camp experiences, Judy answered our yes/no questions about what she did at camp, her smile and laughter indicating that she very much enjoyed the experience. When she came home that first summer, we asked if she wanted to go back again the next year. Her response was an immediate wide-open, jaw-dropping *yes*! Judy knew that camp was good, and she also knew that when it ended, she came home.

So even though she had answered yes when asked if she liked TNH, I believed she was tolerating it until it was time to go home, though I couldn't imagine when she thought that would be. I felt we needed a little more honesty, but I couldn't bear to bluntly tell her that this *was* her home now and she was never going back to the apartment where she had lived before. Instead, I circumvented the issue.

Me: "Remember how Orin and David used to live with us on Davidson Avenue, and then they moved out? And how I used to live at home, and then *my* David came, and he and I moved to our own apartment, and then we moved to a different house?"

Judy: [*bottom lip puckered out*]

Me: "But we still came to visit, and we took you and Mommy places. So it was okay that we went to live somewhere else."

Judy: [*hesitant laugh*]

Me: "Well, now it's *your* turn to move to a new place."

Judy: no response

Me: "And wouldn't TNH be a good place for you to live?"

Judy: [*huge grimace, indicating an unequivocal* no!]

I considered that maybe it wasn't TNH to which she was objecting so much as the idea of leaving her house and living somewhere else permanently. Reasoning that she might be objecting to leaving Mom, I went on to explain, "When children move out, mommies and daddies then live by themselves. It's like me and David living by ourselves now that Ronen, Ilan, and Ari have moved away. So now you can live in a new place, and Mommy will live by herself, and that will be okay." She listened with a continued lack of visible response. I told her to think about it.

I didn't ask Judy again if she would like to live at TNH permanently. I, of course, didn't want another *no* answer, and I did realize that I was asking her as if she had a choice. But I told her that she should think about it because "someday, not so soon, Mommy will be going to stay with Daddy. Remember when Daddy died and he went to a place we call heaven? Well, when Mommy goes to live with him, you will need a new place to live too. The home attendants won't be able to come anymore, and you will need to live someplace where people can take care of you." The only good thing I can say is that Judy seemed to be listening, although mostly passively. She did smile when I mentioned Daddy, and she didn't cry at all. It's very possible that she didn't really understand what I was saying and couldn't imagine a life without my mother, couldn't comprehend what it meant to live permanently at TNH. I'm not sure why I thought I needed to say all that I did, but I guess I was desperate. I so wanted Judy to like TNH, to accept it as her home. I so needed to ease my guilt.

The next few visits were troubling. The day after the "Would you like to live at TNH?" discussion, Judy was crying when I arrived. Then on Monday when I visited with David, we arrived in the middle of dinner. Judy was being fed. She had a bib full of food and just sat in her chair, barely opening her mouth when the food came near. On Tuesday, she was sitting in the dining room waiting for someone to feed her. Her expression was downcast, her head slumped. I under-stood that in any institution, everyone has to wait for attention at some point because there are so many more residents than caregiv-ers. I just wasn't sure that Judy understood that. She started crying. It wasn't loud, and nobody else seemed to notice, or they just weren't paying attention. When the aides saw me, they asked if I was going to feed her. I was glad to do it, but when I tried, Judy didn't seem to want to eat, even with me. She said she wanted to when I asked her, but she kept dropping the food out of her mouth. I thought maybe something was bothering her. I asked her if she had a stomachache or if something in her mouth hurt, but that didn't seem to be the answer. I suddenly realized how terrible it would be for her if she got sick and nobody knew what hurt. She usually cried when she didn't feel well, and Mom would have to try to figure out what was wrong. I couldn't help thinking that if the doctor were right about Judy only living another two years, had we kept her at home, she would have died peacefully in her bed and not suffered the loneliness and distress she now most likely felt. Nor would she have been sick in the care of strangers who couldn't figure out what the problem was and what to do about it.

My emotions swung back and forth like a pendulum. Hope, despair, hope, despair. I sometimes actually felt as if my heart were breaking, shattering like a pane of glass that nothing would ever make whole again. I knew that terrible things happened to good people, but I just couldn't figure out why. *What did Judy ever do? What did any of the people like Judy ever do to deserve a life like this?* It was unbearable for me to see Judy in this place, but it would have been worse not to go see her. When all was said and done, I think I did the right thing—well, the only thing I could have done under the circumstances. But I wondered when it would all end, and I didn't think it would be anytime soon. *What if I die before Judy?* Oh, what a terrible, terrible thought, that she would one day be all alone.

There's a saying about progress that goes something like this: *For every two steps forward, you have to take one step backward.* In my case, it seemed to be: *For every step forward, you take seventeen steps backward.* My shoulders sagged, and my head felt like I needed something to hold it up. The honeymoon was over—and it had been way too short! A day or two of optimism that things were going well, and then back to worry and despair. Despite her previous positive response to David's question about liking TNH, Judy seemed very unhappy. I was ready for this whole thing to end, and I supposed that Judy was feeling the same way. We had tried something new, and now it was time to return to the way things had been. Unfortunately, there *was* no return.

As we tried to settle into a new routine with me visiting when I could after work and David taking Mom to visit Judy on Sundays, David informed me that he had a business trip coming up and would be away for a couple of weeks. That left me needing to transport Mom on those two Sundays. I was willing to do it but had a conflict on one of the Sundays and wouldn't be able to go. I decided I would, once again, turn to my brother for help. I figured he would probably be planning a visit soon anyway, so why not visit on a day when it would be most helpful? I called, and Carrie picked up.

"Hi. Do you think it would be possible for you and Orin to come to pick up Mom and visit Judy on the twenty-fifth?" I explained my problem.

Carrie relayed the request to my brother, and I could hear him in the background asking, "Why?"

Does it matter why?

Carrie relayed my reasons and then replied that they weren't sure—they'd let me know.

Once again, I tried to remember when I had signed up for this solo duty. I had been under the (seemingly mistaken) impression that this was a *family* issue. I understood that Cherry Hill was not down the road. A visit was always a full-day affair for them. David or I, on the other hand, only lost half a day when we visited on a weekend. But the fact that I'd be doing it two or three times a week (not to mention the nearly every day that I'd visited during the prior two weeks) didn't seem to count because I lived closer.

The following week, Orin called to say that he still didn't know if he could come on Sunday, as it would be really difficult for him, especially at that time of year. Fall is always a busy time with the approaching Jewish holidays. I didn't insist—not that it would have mattered. So when he said, "If I *have* to come, I will," I replied that it would be helpful if he could, but if not I would figure something out. We talked about neither of us taking Mom that weekend, but I wasn't happy with that solution. We decided that I would call him the following day, and he would let me know. But as soon as I said it, I already knew I wouldn't call. I felt guilty enough for asking, and I didn't want him to spend a whole day traveling, and so what if I was the one to do it? I didn't like going on a Saturday, but I said I'd switch days and take her then. Orin, likely not intending to add to my distress but increasing my guilt nonetheless, replied, "You know, even though you and David are busy schlepping Mom back and forth in New York, I'm busy schlepping Carrie's mother around from place to place all the time here in New Jersey." I didn't know what to say. I had forgotten that other people had lives and struggles they were dealing with. I had only seen my own.

My brothers were what I always considered typical big brothers. They teased and big-brother bullied me whenever they could. It was part of the ritual of growing up the younger sister. When I was eleven, though, they did something I thought was remarkable. I was spending the summer in the bungalow colony with my family. Mitchell was a friend, and Ross was his slightly younger brother. I don't recall the exact details, only that Ross hit me, and I ran to my bungalow crying. As I sat in my room sobbing, I was visited by each of my brothers in turn. My gentle, normally pacifist brother David said, "You come and tell me if he ever bothers you again, and I'll let him have it! He won't hit you again." He left the room and gave Ross the same message.

My wise, practical brother Orin explained, "If any boy ever goes to hit you, just face him and raise your knee. Jab him right here," he said, pointing to his crotch. "Believe me, he won't hit you again." What a revelation! My brothers were standing up for me, and for the first time in my life, I realized that they loved me. Those small acts of loving protection had a very powerful impact. They were enough to last me a lifetime, and any future teasing and bullying by either of them became insignificant in light of that awareness. This memory made it easier for me to forget my frustration over their lack of assistance with Judy.

On my next visit to Judy, I noticed that the temperature outside was getting cooler. "Next time you will need your poncho." She agreed. The reference to Judy's poncho brought up a fond memory. My mother had been a knitter and enjoyed teaching others. She taught Eulia to knit, and the two of them could be seen with needles and yarn, their fingers deftly moving as they created something for a family member to wear. When it became impossible to get Judy into her coat because her arms had become too rigid to bend easily into the sleeves, the two of them knitted her a poncho and a hat. The poncho was made of several panels that were then sewn together. They used a heavy cotton and knitted it in a tight weave to provide warmth. We would slip the poncho around Judy's shoulders and zip it up, and it covered her upper body and thighs and became a sort of blanket. It and the hat kept Judy warm on many of our cooler-day walks. *I should also get her a small blanket that I can use to cover her legs,* I thought now. *I think I'll look for something special that will be her "walking blanket."* I hoped that, with the addition of the blanket, we would be able to continue our walks at TNH for a while longer. I was trying to plan what we would do when it got too cold to walk, even with the poncho and blanket, but decided not to worry about it because we would ultimately figure something out.

Every time I visited Judy and walked with her down the hallway on our way outside, Maryanne, another resident, came over to talk to me. I wasn't sure why she was at TNH—it seemed to me that there should have been a more appropriate placement for her. She was completely ambulatory. In fact, she seemed to have the run of the building, riding up and down the elevator to the different floors and strolling about on each of the three levels with no clear destination or purpose. She wore an ankle bracelet like those under house arrest, just in case she had ideas about leaving the building. She appeared to be intellectually disabled. I never saw her with a visitor. According to Maryanne, the other residents didn't like her. If that was true, I could understand their annoyance. She talked incessantly and repetitively as she walked up and down the hallway: "Helen lives on the first floor. I saw Helen. Helen lives on the first floor. Do you know Helen? Helen lives on the first floor." And then, on her next pass, "I like the first floor. Helen lives on the first floor. I like the first floor." Or, "I went to the third floor. They play bingo on the third floor. I don't like bingo." And again, "They play bingo on the third floor. I don't like bingo. I went to the first floor. Helen lives on the first floor. Do you know Helen?" And so on. I cringed when she came by to talk to me, as I didn't know what to say to her.

Lisa, on the other hand, required a wheelchair and appeared to me to be higher functioning mentally. Lisa was always offering to help—to watch out for Judy. "Judy was in the hallway, and I said hello." Or, "Judy was lying on her bed, so I came in to talk to her." Actually, on my previous visit she told me that Judy had been laughing earlier that day. That brought a smile to my face. But, as with Maryanne, I tried to avoid her. I felt bad about that, but I had never been much of a conversationalist, so I simply didn't know what to talk to her about. Every time I went, I walked quickly and quietly down the hall, hoping to elude both of them.

When I visited after work, I would arrive just before dinner. A typical visit at this point had Judy already in the dining room with the other residents, waiting to be fed. One day, I could see her from the doorway and I watched her twisting in her chair, calling for attention. *Oh, how Judy hates to wait!* My body tensed, and my stomach knotted. *I wish she could learn to wait her turn calmly.* But I knew it was hard for her. Determined not to let it upset me, I suddenly understood. *This is Judy's way of telling those around her that she is ready to eat, that she doesn't like to wait and wants them to hurry. This is Judy talking.*

Journal Entry
September 29, 2005
My thoughts are constantly racing, both when I'm on my way to TNH and when I return home. Once I open the door and enter my house, however, I am safe once again and, faced with the responsibilities of home and work preparation, the racing recedes into the background of my mind. I suppose it's good that I can get some respite, though I am sorry to lose the reflections I have on my journeys back and forth. Tonight I'll take the time to write them down before they slip away.

The best thing about the trip to TNH is the getting there and back— the drive. In fact, it is the drive that gets me through the roughest days. Never any traffic, so I can glide on my way. And it is so beautiful. I counted six little bridges I go over. On sunny days, the sun reflects off the water. How calming and serene water can be! It is spacious and open and reminds me each time of the wonders of G-d's creation. Tonight the sky was outstanding. Most of the way there, I drove into the pink-and-blue swirls made by the clouds. To the side, where the sun had already begun to set, the bright orange that remained lit up what had earlier been a blue sky. The other side held the same pink and blue of the clouds, as they stretched across the horizon. I would like to say that driving through this beauty makes it all worthwhile, but nothing could do that. It makes it bearable, though. And it is a part that I actually look forward to. Picture it: Nature's beauty. Life's therapy. I'll take whatever I can get!

As I drive up and park the car, I enter TNH with a mixture of dread and happy anticipation. I always look forward to seeing Judy. This whole experience has brought out feelings previously obscured by having a family of my own. It is good to be reminded how much I love my sister. The special bond of twinship that I have always felt is something that can never be broken. The dread I feel on entering TNH is from knowing what awaits me inside. The place is the same; the people don't change. My sister is there, and there she will remain. What's not to dread?

My dismay comes from the shame of abandonment: I didn't watch over Judy when she was at home. I didn't speak up or encourage my mother to speak up and make the agency send people who would be more involved. I didn't visit as often as I might have when she lived at home. In short, she stopped being the most important person in my life. By failing to be vigilant, I let the situation at home decline so that we are where we are today. Now I want so much to ease her sorrow, and instead I feel that I am the cause of it. She looks so sad when I leave. I put her in her room and put on her tape. She no longer cries—at least not on the outside. I cry—on the inside. Nevertheless I am happy to leave, to escape, to run away to a place where I can be safe from the sadness. But I cannot escape the guilt. The guilt lives within me always.

7
Things Change, Anxieties Remain

It is very interesting how a human mind works. Leaving TNH on my visits to Judy, I would be bursting to share that day's story in my journal. By the time I got home, however, I was just too tired to sit myself down to write. The next day the normalcy of my life would return, and the need to vent would recede into the background. People who hadn't heard from me in a while would call and ask how things were going, and I didn't quite know what to say. Before TNH, my answer to such a question might have been, "Fine, nothing new," but now I was tempted to reply, "Sucky, nothing new," though I stuck to "Fine," as I didn't want to sound like I was complaining.

Although nothing had changed inside TNH, the weather outside was changing, and that threatened to change the substance of my visits. Judy had gotten into the routine of taking a walk outside whenever one of us came to visit, and Judy was very definitely a *routine* person. She relied on set patterns, much as a child does. The predictability of set routines helps both children and adults with disabilities feel safe in their environment. It gives them a sense of security in knowing what to expect. So I was reluctant to change the routine we had established at TNH, and I continued walking with Judy as fall settled in, even taking little walks in the rain. I worried, though, that walking outside couldn't go on much longer, and one day I told her that we'd have to come up with another plan. I always felt the need to explain things to Judy, as it helped her prepare for what lay ahead. Even though she had no choice about any of it, I felt it was disrespectful to simply do things that affected her life without letting her know what was happening and why.

The new routine began with our going out to the patio and walking around for a few minutes on bad weather days. Judy didn't like being cold and wet and would twist and grunt if she was uncomfortable, so the short patio walks were enough for her. She would start out sitting, her body relaxed, and when she started twisting and making her unhappy grunting noises, I knew it was time to go in. Still, it was clear that when it got too cold for even those walks, I would need a new routine yet again, something that we could do together that would take the place of the long walks we were accustomed to sharing. In addition to a routine, I was looking for a way to connect, and I realized that a lot of what I liked about our walks was having the opportunity to talk to her. I loved telling her stories because she always listened and often laughed. Who doesn't love an appreciative audience? As I often arrived at TNH close to her dinnertime and found it too quiet while I fed her, I thought I could tell Judy accounts of my day, thereby transferring my storytelling from our walks to dinner. Conversation with Judy may have been mainly one-sided, but my talking to her allowed me to feel the connection I was looking for. I gave it a try during dinner one evening, going through the details of what I had done that day, telling the story as one would tell a small child.

"The alarm clock went off this morning, and I jumped up really fast to shut it off. I almost fell off the bed! My foot got caught in the blanket, and I pulled and twisted and pulled and twisted. The alarm was sooo loud, and I didn't want it to wake David because then he would be grumpy all day. I finally got my foot out and managed not to fall on the floor . . ."

Judy was engaged, watching me speak as she opened and closed her mouth over the food I scooped in. I thought, *This is good. She likes it. I think this could work!* Alas, it worked so well in engaging her that she started to laugh. Laughing and eating don't go well together, and before I knew it, Judy was laughing so hard she started coughing, and food spouted out everywhere. Sadly, I realized that dinner wasn't a good time for conversation. I stopped my storytelling and resumed it when she'd finished eating. Unfortunately, she was no longer interested and started twisting, impatient for a new activity. I would have to keep thinking and hopefully come up with something else.

At around that time, Erika's mother told me that she had plans for Erika to be moving out of TNH in two years to go into an Individualized Residential Alternative (IRA) program. IRAs are group homes whose focus is to promote independent living while providing services based on the needs of its residents, supervised around the clock by trained staff. They were beginning to open up to more severely impaired people than previously, and Erika now qualified. Not fully understanding the parameters required for acceptance into the program, I dared to think that maybe Judy would be eligible. Though I was thrilled for Erika and her mother, the thought of Erika leaving, even in two years, upset me. I, like Judy, was a creature of habit, and once I got used to something, I found change difficult. At the same time, hearing that Erika would be moving gave me hope that Judy might not be doomed to live in TNH for the rest of her life and would, perhaps, one day be able to enjoy life in a smaller, more pleasant residence. As it would be two years before Erika could move, I figured it would be a long time before anything would happen for Judy. That time factor was a real damper for me as I wondered how long I could continue visiting TNH over an extended period of time. How long could I continue to walk through those foul-smelling halls, surrounded by people whose lives were defined by their disability? How long could I suffer the despair of seeing my sister in such a place? Already, less than two months felt like eternity. TNH had been depressing when Judy arrived, it was depressing now, and I guessed that it would be depressing always.

Often when we feel things are out of control, we find something we *can* take charge of. To regain a sense of agency over what was happening, I decided to consult an attorney about becoming Judy's legal guardian. Perhaps it was being her twin that caused me to feel responsible for her, that I alone most understood and knew what was best for her. For all of my life, I felt she was my other half, and protecting her was, in a sense, protecting myself. I didn't know if I would ever need legal guardianship, but I wanted to take precautions in case future decisions had to be made. Legal guardianship would mean that my permission would be necessary if medical care was needed. It would also allow me to make decisions regarding Judy's life, such as having her moved to another placement—possibly an IRA. I wasn't sure that Mom would be capable of making these decisions, and I wanted to be prepared.

I found out from the lawyer that Mom could put money in a trust for Judy, and that money would only be accessible by her family, to be used solely for Judy—clothing, a TV, a trip to Hawaii, anything really—and Judy would still qualify for Medicaid and Medicare. She had been receiving benefits from the Social Security Administration since she was twenty-one, and those benefits now paid for her stay at TNH. Any extra money that was being spent on Judy (such as clothing) came from my mother. A trust fund would be very helpful in allaying those expenses.

Taking control in another area, I began allowing myself to skip visits. Judy had, at this point, never been more than a day without a visitor. Then came the day when I had planned to go but didn't. It wasn't because it was pouring rain, though that did make my decision more bearable. It wasn't because I nearly fell asleep during staff development, because I knew I would wake up once I started driving—my concern about the roads would have kept me awake. It wasn't even because David and my mother would be going the following day. I didn't go because the timing would have been bad. I got ahead of myself in my mind and built up the scenario of what *might* happen. Staff development at work ended at three o'clock, so I would have gotten to Judy at three forty-five. She would still be on the bed, possibly sleeping. *Should I then wake her? If I do, then what?* I worried. *She'll be expecting me to put her in her chair so we can take our walk. I don't think the weather will allow for even a two-minute walk on the patio today. Where can we walk that will satisfy her? Will a walk in the hallways be good enough?* I worried. *And taking a walk earlier than usual would mean my putting her in the chair. But I can't do that with-out changing her diaper.* The aides didn't like it when I changed Judy's diaper because then they couldn't keep track of her "eliminations." *I will have to ask the aide to put her in the chair. But first I will have to find the aide.* I felt like a character in *If You Give a Mouse a Cookie* (by Laura Numeroff, 1985). But the book was written for children and filled with humor, while this "getting ahead of myself" was causing a growing anxiety. *My other option is to leave her on the bed and try to keep her satisfied until the aide comes in to put her in the chair. Then, of course, I'll have to find someplace to walk, and then it will be time for dinner, and I'll have to feed her.*

Getting there before four o'clock and staying until after dinner meant that I would be there longer than I wanted. I remember con-sidering a possible scenario that I would get there while she was on the bed and I would explain to her that I was just going to have a very short visit today. Then we could talk while she was on the bed, and if the aide came in, maybe I'd stay for a short walk down the hallway and bring her to the dining room, where the aide would give her dinner, and I would leave. I suspected she would start tensing up and making complaining noises if I left without first giving her dinner. I knew she wouldn't really understand why I couldn't stay and feed her, so I would end up doing just that. The anxiety created by all this presupposing made my head spin. It was exhausting!

In the end, instead of going on my visit and simply letting things just play out, I opted for the easy way out and stayed home. The guilt of not going at all seemed more palatable than the discomforting thought of being in that place for any longer than I had to be, and even through the guilt, I felt the tension leave my body. I was okay with the decision. Knowing that David and Mom would be visiting the next day definitely helped, but it was also an out-of-sight, out-of-mind phenomenon. I understood that Judy enjoyed our visits—she liked us to feed her, to take her for a walk, to break the monotony. She needed to see the familiar faces of those who love her and to be reassured that we hadn't totally abandoned her. When I thought of her being there without visitors, I thought of her being sad, but thinking is one thing and seeing is another. If I couldn't *see* her being sad, I allowed myself to think, *Maybe she isn't really sad.* I never asked any of Judy's aides if they noticed a sadness. I'm not sure if it was because I felt so sure that I knew what she was feeling or because I was afraid to have my suspicions confirmed. I didn't ask, and except for one or two occasions when an aide mentioned that Judy had been sitting quietly in the rec room, no one offered. I also didn't know if Judy was able to keep track of the days, so I didn't think she said to herself, *Well, Debbie hasn't visited in two days, so she'll probably come today.* I think she just went along with TNH's routine. And so if I didn't come one day, it was no different from the day before, when I also didn't come. I did consider that this new attitude of mine would ultimately "allow" me to visit less, and that made me feel really sad for Judy, though not enough to overcome my dread of being at TNH.

My anxieties started affecting my sleep, and I began to have disturbing dreams. I dreamed that it was Passover and my niece had already arrived for the seder, but I hadn't finished the extensive preparations. In the dream, I was in a panic. Had it been April at Passover time, this dream would have made sense, but in October it was strange. The prior night, I'd dreamed about Judy. She was home for a visit, and my cousins from Washington and their kids and grandkids had come to see her. They all sat on one side of the living room, and Judy sat in her chair at the other end. She was young and sat relaxed, holding her head up well. She looked "normal" except that she was in a wheelchair. My cousins, who in reality rarely visited at all, had come to see Judy, but no one was paying any attention to her. Only I noticed her sitting there in her chair. I wondered what the dream meant. I could only think that all the disturbing dreams I was having were a subconscious result of the apprehensions I was feeling when I was awake.

As the days grew shorter, my anxiety only worsened. The thought of driving to TNH in the dark frightened me. I knew I wouldn't be able to see the water as I went over the bridges, and I depended on those "life-affirming" visuals. They were what gave me strength each time I visited.

There came a week when I was off from school for several days and I was able to make two daytime visits. Both days were very sunny and somewhat warm, and we were able to take our walk. We passed a library and, on the way back one time, we stopped in. Judy had never been to a library before. She kept her head up and looked at all the books as we walked around. We took out a children's book about autumn leaves. I tried reading it when we got back to her room. She allowed it without twisting or complaining but only because we had to wait for the aide to fix her bed before she could take her rest. She barely looked at the pictures. I wished that she would be more interested in my reading to her. That would have given me the connection I was looking for, and it was something that I enjoyed doing. I remembered how, when we were little, I used to read to Judy all the time. Reading was just a part of the special relationship we had in those days, when Judy was my pal. We did so many things together. Then, as we got older, and I married and had children, my own family became my priority, and that pal relationship got lost. Possibly because it was no longer part of her routine, she now showed no interest in my reading or playing games with her. Now all I could think of to do was take her for walks. Why is it that we often look back on life and think how much easier it used to be, but at the time we didn't see it that way at all?

Journal Entry
October 15, 2005

Anyone who knows me knows that I do not walk around morose, with my head down, unable to smile and unresponsive to the joy that goes on around me. At least I do not perceive myself in that light. Yet that is the portrait that I feel I paint for myself in this journal. I suppose it is because the purpose—or benefit—of the writing is to vent my frustrations. When I write, I look into my soul and bring out those thoughts that I otherwise try to keep buried. This is such a sad period in my life, but the sadness is not all of who I am. I wish I could find that other self, my happier self. I often fear that she is lost forever.

I've generally thought of myself as a pretty patient person. Knowing there's an end to something has gotten me through many difficult points in my life—from writing school papers to childbirth and from the terrible twos to adolescent children. Not knowing that there will ever be an end to this episode of my life is extremely challenging for me. When I think of the years ahead at TNH, I can't bear it. Judy gets so excited every time David, my mom, or I come to visit. She laughs so loud, everyone around her is astounded. It's wonderful that she's so happy to see us, but all it really says to me is how unhappy she is the rest of the time. I don't know if I have it in me to feel her sadness multiple times a week for the rest of my life. Oh, when I think of all those people who have been in this place for so many years! It is just so distressing. In twenty years, Judy and I will be seventy-three years old. No reason to think we both won't still be alive. Is this all that we have to look forward to?

I may have once written that this experience has made a hole in my heart. It is as if there is a spot in my heart, maybe the size of a half-dollar, that is continuously pressed in while, all around it, my heart continues to beat. It is just there. It doesn't interfere with the function of my heart, but that section does not beat. It remains pressed in. I think that spot has died and will remain pressed in evermore.

8

Turmoil

As time went on, people would ask me how my mother and Judy were doing. I didn't really know how to answer, though I generally responded, "They seem to be doing okay." I wanted to believe that was true, and yet I also wondered, *Are they really doing okay?* On the outside, they were. My mother was taking care of herself and said that her once-a-week visits were enough. Judy no longer cried—at least not that I was aware of—and seemed to have adjusted to her routine. But what about on the inside? *What is my mother thinking that she doesn't tell me? And what is Judy thinking that she is unable to share with* anyone?

On the outside, I, too, was doing fine, wasn't I? I went to work, did my job, talked to my friends, came home to David, talked to my kids, and took care of my house. My life continued. I coped. But I wasn't really okay. I believed that my sadness should have gone away by that point and that I should have been feeling better, accepting the situation. I wanted to be strong, to persevere, but I couldn't seem to get better. It was that heaviness, that hollow part of my heart. I didn't want it anymore, but it wouldn't go away. It made me so tired.

I knew I was no different from anyone else. Everyone has worries; only the details are different. No one goes through life without challenges of some sort, but when they are *ours*, they can feel very big. My own struggles continued to be connected to the logistics involved in my visits. The succession of thoughts going through my head at the time included:

It's really bad weather, so I won't be able to take Judy for a walk.

I could go anyway and feed her and walk around inside.

Even when I can visit during the day, I don't love walking around—mostly because people in wheelchairs are always blocking my path, and I have to ask them to move, which takes them so long that I don't know if I should move them or let them do it themselves, and the whole thing makes me so uncomfortable.

I'm finding that I don't really enjoy feeding Judy. I once found it gratifying, a pleasurable opportunity to help out and connect with her, but now it's a chore. Is it because it takes so long, or because I'm uncomfortable with the silence? I feel that I can't talk because then she ends up coughing and gagging.

Well, I could get there after she's already eaten, but will she be disappointed? And I'll still have to take her for a walk.

I could try my new idea of reading to her, but I don't know if that will work, and for some reason, I'm afraid to try. Well, I actually did try about a month ago, when I brought in a book and told her that we could read like we did when we were little. I got to the first page, and she wouldn't let me continue. I felt rejected. I think that's why I'm afraid of trying again.

If I wait until tomorrow, when the weather is better, I'll be able to take Judy for a walk outside.

If I don't go today, it will mean that I only go once this week. That's not being a good sister. Oh, I want so much to be a good sister, and I'm just not living up to the task. I'm crying now. Feeling sorry for myself and sorry for Judy that she doesn't have someone better than me. But it doesn't change my mind. The bottom line is, I don't want to go. And so I've found an excuse, and I've made my decision. I'll go tomorrow. Tomorrow is always better. Facing things tomorrow is always easier than facing them today.

No, I was definitely *not* doing well on the inside.

I have always done my most introspective thinking in the shower. Before TNH, my shower thoughts were often of Judy and what would happen with her as my mother aged further, and how my mother would respond when ultimately Judy was placed in a home. After her placement in TNH, my thoughts of Judy expanded to outside the shower and throughout the day. I was obsessing. I couldn't stop worrying.

Meanwhile, the visits continued. We kept walking, and I fed her when the timing was right, which was during most of my visits. On one such visit, she didn't eat very well, and I noticed she had a lot of extra saliva in her mouth. I kept trying to wipe it away, but it was gooey and persistent, and it seemed to be making it difficult for her to swallow. When I told the nurse that Judy had eaten very little, she said, "Maybe she just ate a lot for lunch." She wasn't concerned about the saliva, but I was bothered by it and also by the fact that the nurse dismissed it. To me, anything irregular was important, and the nurse's lack of concern was frustrating. I wanted to trust the medical professionals, and at the same time, I wanted them to listen to me, to hear and respond to my concerns, and to recognize that I knew my sister better than they did.

On another visit, after one of our walks, I put Judy on the bed and noticed that she needed her diaper changed. I told the nurse, who said she would send an aide. Forty-five minutes (and two additional requests) later, the aide came in. If you knew how hard it is for me to ask for something, you would know how uncomfortable I was asking *three* times, however politely. I didn't want to upset someone who might take out their resentment toward me on Judy. So I waited the forty-five minutes, although I wasn't happy. If I hadn't been there, however, she probably would have waited even longer—until the aide came in at around a quarter past four to put her in the chair for dinner. Unfortunately, Judy can't regulate her bodily functions to their schedule.

As the weeks passed, my husband David continued his weekend visits with my mother, but they started taking a toll on him. In addition to the round trips from Long Island to TNH via Queens, he was beginning to be bothered by the hallway smells and the number of disabled residents congregating in the hallways on his Sunday visits. It came to a head one Sunday when Judy was being nudgy during the visit, emitting negative grunting sounds. We always found this behavior frustrating because we could see that she wanted something but didn't know what it was. That day, David had taken Judy for a walk and then brought her back for lunch. She was kvetching and twisting her head and indicated that she wanted to go into the dining room. David thought she liked eating in there. I wasn't sure. She always looked toward the door to her room and became distracted by what was going on in the hall when I fed her. He brought her into the dining room and she seemed content, but visitors were not allowed to feed the residents in there, so David returned Judy to her room, allowing my mother to give her lunch.

In general, David didn't like watching my mother feed Judy because Judy would drop the food out of her mouth, and my mother didn't seem to notice, so it ended up making a mess. He would leave the room and come back when he thought she'd be finished. That particular day, though, everything bothered him—the feeding, the kvetching, the foul odors, and the overall chaos brought about by all the weekend visitors. He said he didn't think he could continue to visit every week. I sympathized completely. I didn't go on the weekend because I couldn't deal with the number of people. More wheelchairs in the halls—the increase due to the residents who were not out at a day program—made it harder to walk, longer to wait for the elevator, more noise, more everything.

David had already spoken to Grace's son Eddie, who was now staying with Mom at night. A college student, Eddie had evidently been looking to move out of his family's home, and Grace had suggested that he take her place in Mom's apartment, making sure she didn't do anything dangerous like leave the fire burning under the teakettle. It was working out nicely, and they were developing a pleasant relationship. David had asked Eddie if he would be willing to drive my mother on Saturdays. He had tried several times to explain to

Mom that all the driving was difficult for him, and he would look for someone else to drive her. Eddie said he would be willing, but when he mentioned it to my mother, she told him that it wasn't necessary because David drove her. David said he would speak to Mom again, but I worried that if Eddie brought her, my mother would be on her own once she got there, and I wasn't sure she'd be able to handle it. For one thing, she wouldn't be able to take Judy for a walk. It was simply too physically difficult for her to push the chair outside. And I didn't know if my mother would think to walk her around the hallway or if she would be able to walk long enough to satisfy Judy. Also, if one of the nurses or aides had to tell her something, would she remember what the nurse said—or even hear it?

As it turned out, on one visit, Mom asked a nurse about getting Judy a haircut. "Judy's hair is very long. Is there anyone here who can give her a haircut?" The nurse said a hairdresser came once a month, and she would add Judy's name to the list. The next visit, and the one after that, included the same question and the same answer. I wasn't sure whether Mom kept asking because she was being persistent or because she had forgotten that she'd already asked. I thought it was the latter. Finally, the hairdresser came, and Judy had her haircut. My mother was pleased, and I was happy that she didn't have to ask about it anymore. I should have realized that Mom was still capable of noticing what needed to be done and taking care of it, even if it did seem like her forgetfulness was getting in the way. In fact, it was more productive than my method of not speaking up and hoping that whatever needed to happen would occur sooner or later.

I was also concerned, though, that Mom didn't always pay attention to what was going on around her in TNH. She didn't remember the aides or the other residents, and she didn't understand how things worked, like the need to get Judy's food tray in order to feed her in her room, for instance. Her routine was to go straight to Judy's room and wait for David to take Judy for a walk, then feed Judy when David brought the tray. After that she'd be tired and ready to go home. I was worried that if her routine changed and Eddie brought her there, she would forget that David wasn't taking her home and that she would have to go downstairs and find Eddie and would, instead, just sit waiting in Judy's room while Eddie sat and waited downstairs in his car. I didn't feel comfortable leaving her to deal with all this by herself, though I'm not sure why I didn't realize that Eddie could easily go upstairs and get Mom. We could have arranged for Eddie to bring her and I would meet her there, but I couldn't bring myself to go there on the weekend. So instead of Eddie driving, I suggested that David go every other week, and that would have to be enough for my mother. If not, and I had to go on alternate weekends, I would. At least I would try.

Though David's growing dislike of being at TNH threatened to create logistical issues that I didn't want to deal with, it felt good that we were on the same page now in our feelings toward the place. I not only felt somehow vindicated, but the weight of the obligation seemed lighter because he shared my perspective. I was spending two afternoons a week visiting Judy and a tremendous amount of time and energy just *thinking* about her and all that was going on—time that could otherwise have been spent on school or housework. The time it took me to write down my thoughts at the end of the day also took time away from other work, but writing allowed me to release some of my feelings. Being able to let go of pent-up feelings actually frees the mind and allows for more productivity, so I hoped it would work that way for me. I started making to-do lists for the upcoming week—a good way to keep tabs on what was most important. At the end of each week, I would transfer to my new list at least half of what I didn't get to the week before, but I was glad to see that I actually was accomplishing some tasks. At the same time, though, I felt I was falling further and further behind. I kept telling myself, *This is temporary. It will get better.* I just wasn't convinced.

I hated to admit this, but on weekends, when I didn't have to visit Judy, I woke up relaxed, stress-free, and eager to begin my day. I only felt my body tense up and my smile fade when I thought of the possibility that I might have to relieve David and start going on alternate

Sundays, and tears welled up in my eyes as I agonized over this. In the beginning, I looked forward to seeing Judy and being able to spend time with her, and she had been so excited when I arrived. After a while, though, seeing her didn't bring me joy because she seemed so sad, and her excitement at seeing *me* was no longer evident. Was an opportunity to go for a walk the only value my visits had for her? I remembered the times when David and I would bring the kids to my mother's apartment for dinner every Friday evening. We would enter the house, and if we didn't go straight in to see her, within minutes Judy would be laughing or making noises to get our attention—as if to say, *Hey, where are you guys? I'm waiting! Come in and say hello!* She would greet us with a laugh and a big smile as we made some joke like, "We're coming as fast as we can. You wouldn't want us to trip and fall, would you?" I missed Judy's laughter. I missed her enthusiasm.

Journal Entry
November 12, 2005

When I speak to my brother Orin and his wife, Carrie, they ask how things are. I think I say something like, "Fine, I guess," or "I guess it's going okay." Today's shower thoughts included my feelings about this. Can I expect my brother to understand what I'm going through if I am not honest with him about my feelings? Obviously not! So I think it's time that I stop skirting around the issue with him and his family. Maybe it's important that they all know what goes on in my head. Maybe it would help with those feelings of resentment I'd rather not have. So what will I say? I want to explain that my life is pretty sucky right now, and I don't see it getting better—ever—and that, for whatever reason, Judy has become my responsibility, and it's not fair.

I want to express what it's like to think every day about when I will go to see Judy and what time I should get there and what we will do once I get there, and that I have to see all those people, and I have to walk with her in the hall and pass through the line of wheelchairs. I would like to talk about how I can't even plan a vacation without thinking about how many days I can skip seeing Judy, and how, when I look at my future, I see Judy growing old at TNH and me, older as well, slowly walking down the corridor on my way to visit her.

The only one who makes it possible for me to wake up every day and face my life is my husband David, who goes far and beyond what any brother-in-law should have to do. He is my savior, and whether they know it or not, he is their savior too. I want to tell my family that I'm aware that life often isn't fair and that everyone has their problems to deal with, but I also want them to know that, right now and as far as my mind can see, life sucks for me. And when I've said all I need to say, I don't want them to respond. I'm not looking for anyone to feel sorry for me or to solve my problems—just to be aware that they exist and that, to me at least, they're big. Now the question is, will I have the guts to say it?

9
The Truth Comes Out

I am in awe of people who have major issues to deal with every day and yet continue to manage their lives. I have a friend like that. Life hasn't always been kind to her, but she doesn't let it get her down. She faces the challenges head-on.

I know that stress is a natural part of life; some people just deal with it better than others, and I wasn't doing so well at handling the challenges life was presenting me. *After all,* I told myself, *my Judy situation is just on top of all the other, ordinary life stresses I face.* First, there was my family. My children were all on their way to becoming adults, and while that is what every parent wants, there's something bittersweet about the loss of *child* identities. My oldest, Ronen, was in Boston attending law school. I felt his stress over the demands for long hours of study and high performance on exams, and the dilemma of whether to take a part-time job. Ilan, my middle child, was struggling to figure out who he was and what direction to take in his life. My youngest, Ari, was trying to adjust to living away from home, dealing with the normal demands of college, and trying to maintain a social life as he said goodbye to his teenage years and entered into his twenties. They were rarely all home at the same time, and I felt our sense of family beginning to fall apart.

I didn't confide in them much about Judy being in TNH because I didn't want them to see me as anything but the strong, stable mother I wanted to be. In addition, I was always afraid that if something happened to me, the responsibility for looking after Judy would go to them. By not sharing all that was going on, I somehow thought I was protecting them. Looking back, I realize I should have confided in them, shared my struggles. Aside from teaching the lesson that life isn't always easy, even for adults, it most likely would have brought us more of that closeness that I feared was slipping away. As for the rest of my family, I wondered how much longer David would be able to visit Judy, as his aversion to TNH grew with each visit. And Mom was becoming more forgetful and seemed to be having difficulty understanding her new situation in life. Her sense of time was now pretty much nonexistent, and she tired quickly. I sensed that this unwanted change in her life played a role in her decline.

At work, I wanted so much to make a difference in the lives of the children I taught. That was nothing new, but I was afraid I might be falling short because I was often preoccupied with worries about Judy and Mom.

A year earlier, I had started a master's program in supervision and administration at Bank Street College in Manhattan. I was working at a slower-than-snail's pace on my course assignments and feared that the project I had chosen for my thesis had little chance of being successful if I couldn't give it my all. The project, "The Introduction of Literacy Centers into a Half-Day General Studies Program," was especially challenging because it took place in a Jewish day school where half the day was spent on general studies in English, and the other half focused on Hebrew language and Judaic studies, giving teachers half the time to teach what the public schools taught in a full school day. I worked with a second-grade teacher in her classroom and met with her outside of school hours to plan and evaluate. I only hoped the fatigue caused by the stress and worry I was feeling about TNH and Judy wasn't interfering with my ability to concentrate on my work.

In the meantime, I was eating poorly, snacking all day long, and getting little exercise. My right shoulder began to hurt, the pain running down my arm, as emotional stress took a toll on my physical health.

I remember attending the funeral of a parent of three young children at my school. I had heard that Mr. Z's death was imminent. He had been ill for about two years. The teachers in the school all knew it was coming. Even before the highly emotional funeral, I was experiencing sleepless nights. In addition to being so terribly upset for the family, for all they had been through and would yet have to endure, the experience opened up a flood of unrest within me. It was concrete evidence that people have problems bigger than mine. So I began to question whether I had a right to my feelings of distress and frustration. Rationally, I understood that everyone is entitled to their feelings. There is no wrong way to feel. Yet I wondered, *What gives me the right to complain while others around me have it just as hard, or harder?* I felt guilty that my problems seemed small compared to others, and yet, to me, they were overwhelming. I wanted to be able to cope better, to take what was handed to me and keep moving, but I couldn't. I was stuck feeling sorry for myself and wondering, *What kind of person does that make me?* I wished it would all just go away.

On one of my visits to Judy, she was on the bed when I arrived. This was unusual because at that hour, she should have been in the dining room finishing up dinner. I was confused and, of course, she offered no enlightenment. When I asked her, "Judy, did you have your supper already?" she didn't respond.

Just as I was getting ready to go ask the nurse if I could put her in the chair for a walk, an aide came in with her food. I wasn't happy that I had to feed her, but I put her in the chair and she ate well enough, so it worked out. Toward the end of the meal, she started kvetching, and I assumed it was because she wanted to go for her walk. I took the tray back to the dining room, and when I returned, we started on our walk, but she continued kvetching. I thought it was because she wanted to go out or maybe to a different floor (David did that), but I reminded her that I didn't like taking the elevator, and it was okay to only walk on the second floor. Her kvetching didn't stop, and I couldn't figure out why. It was just so frustrating that she couldn't tell me what she wanted. When we passed one of the aides, I told her that I'd been surprised to find Judy on the bed when I got there. "We were told to keep Judy on the bed and not to put her in the chair," she said. When I asked why, the frustrating response I received was, "I don't know why."

Wouldn't you think they would tell the aides what was going on with their patients? At school, when there was a concern about a child, we would meet as a team and discuss possible actions we might take. Shouldn't the same principle of sharing information apply in Judy's setting? I went looking for answers. James, the head nurse, explained, "Judy has a sore on her shoulder and one on her lower back, so we're keeping her on the bed as much as possible." Partly because of the deterioration of her spine, and partly because the aides weren't seating her in the chair properly, Judy had been more slouched when she sat in her chair, and her shoulder began rubbing against the chair wing that was meant to help keep her head up, something I had previously brought to their attention. This was another example of how frustrating it can be when a family member knows more than the professionals and the professionals aren't listening. James added, "It's okay for her to be in the chair some of the time, but not for too long." With that, I figured out why Judy had been kvetchy—she was telling me that she was supposed to go back on the bed after dinner!

So after our walk, I put her back on the bed and got her set up with the TV. One of the residents, Susie, came in to say hello to her. This was someone I saw all the time but had never spoken to. Judy was twisting her head back, facing some pictures I had put up on the wall, as if trying to show them to Susie. I knew that wasn't the reason she was twisting, but I showed Susie the photographs, including a baby picture of Judy and me. Susie looked at it, smiled, and said, "I have a twin sister too." She unsteadily put out her hand for me to shake, indicating that we were "sisters" in our twinship. I shook it, aware that it was not uncommon for one in a set of twins to have some sort of disability. In that unfortunate statistic, I was not unique. I had heard about disabilities in twins years earlier when Judy and I were children. We had been participants in a study on twins being conducted by Dr. S, her doctor at the time. I remember going into the city to his office where they weighed and measured us. The doctor explained that he was studying twins where one of the twins was disabled because it was fairly common, and he wanted to find out more about it. I don't remember any follow-up visits, and though I often wondered about it, I never found out if the study was ever completed. Now, in Judy's room at TNH, a short conversation with Susie followed the handshake, and I was pleased that I understood her speech. Susie went back to her room, and I left Judy contentedly watching TV. I went home feeling good. I guess it doesn't take much!

I tried to talk myself into generally being in a more positive mood. Though this visit had ended well, I usually didn't succeed, and when I felt a visit was not a good one, I would end up crying the whole way home. On one such visit, I got to TNH late, intentionally, so I wouldn't have to feed Judy. I was expecting to see her sitting down the hall by the nurses' station. Instead, she sat alone halfway down the hall, quite isolated. She had her eyes closed, her face in a grimace, and was twisting her head and shoulders around in her seat—clearly unhappy. The hole in my heart just got bigger, and I fought hard to hold back my own tears.

It took me several minutes to get a hold of myself. After we did our second-floor walk, up and down the hall several times, we stopped in her room to "talk," allowing me a small break. I just couldn't face Bobby, Judy's across-the-hall neighbor, one more time. After all, how many times can I walk up and down the same hallway, responding to Bobby's repeated inquiry, "Do you have any questions for me?" How many times can I ask the question I know he most wants to answer, "Bobby, what will you be doing for Thanksgiving?" He was so excited that he would be going home for the holiday, it was inevitable that when he saw me with Judy, he would ask if Judy was going to be doing the same. Judy's eyes got teary and she pouted, her lower lip protruding, her face scrunched up and looking ready to cry, when I answered, "No, she's going to stay here." I turned to Judy and said, "Not everyone will be going home for the holiday," and even though I knew it was highly unlikely, added, "Maybe some other holiday you'll go home." She continued to pout but relaxed her face when I assured her, "There will be plenty of people here to take care of you. You won't be here alone." Naturally, a whole new layer of guilt got added to the preexisting one already heavy on my shoulders. Just the thought of bringing Judy home, even for a day, seemed overwhelmingly complicated. For one thing, going to New Jersey, where we usually went for Thanksgiving, would be out of the question, and it was too taxing for Mom to host, so I would have to have done it. In my house, Judy would either have to be upstairs on someone's bed while everyone else was eating and talking downstairs, or she would have to lie on the couch in the living room next to the extended dining table, which wasn't always so comfortable for her.

The thought of her lying on the couch brought up the memory of the last Passover seder Judy attended at my house. Judy was given her supper in her chair when she arrived, and when the seder began, she was put on the couch. The first few years that we did this, Judy seemed content to be on the couch listening to the singing. Then we started noticing that, after lying quietly for a few minutes, she would start complaining and was clearly uncomfortable. That last year, we ended up putting her on a bed upstairs shortly after the seder began, and she really wasn't a part of it at all. The following year, Judy stayed at home with her home attendant, and Mom came alone. Though Judy had once enjoyed family gatherings, as she got older she had less patience for the chatter, probably exacerbated by being uncomfortable in her chair for lengthy periods of time. As all these memories floated through my mind, I realized that though bringing Judy home for Thanksgiving presented logistical problems, the most salient argument against Judy coming home for Thanksgiving or any holiday was that when it was over, we would have to take her back. I didn't think any of us, particularly Judy, would be able to handle that.

When it was time for me to leave, I told Judy that we would do one last walk around and then I would bring her to her room and set up the TV. She was relaxed when I said it, but as soon as we got back to her room, she made her complaining noise. "You're not ready to go on the bed?" She grimaced no. So I ended up taking her for one more hallway walk, then brought her to her room, turned on the TV, and said goodbye. She was still complaining, but I couldn't figure out why. I sat with her for a few more minutes and then left her there and stood outside where she couldn't see me to make sure she didn't cry, but Bobby started telling me about Thanksgiving again and I was afraid she would hear me talking, so I left, thinking all the while about how awful it was for her to be alone in this place.

With Thanksgiving approaching, I made the decision to tell my extended family how things really were with me. I wanted to set them straight, so that when they asked, "How are you?" and "How's Judy doing?" they would really know. I was no longer going to do the "I'm fine, everything's fine, Judy's doing pretty well" routine. So when Thanksgiving came, I went to dinner with the resolve that I wouldn't leave with them not knowing.

Well, that was the plan.

No one asked when I arrived. No one asked while we stood around before the meal. No one asked during the meal. I decided I wasn't going to say anything after all. I didn't want to be the one to ruin the happy mood. *Maybe I'll write them all a letter.* Then, after dinner, I walked into the kitchen, and my mother was talking to Carrie's sister, Brenda, saying something like, "Well, she seems to be adjusting." I cringed. There it was again—the big misconception. Not that my mother was lying. I'd even had a hand in convincing her that Judy *was* adjusting, remarking, "Judy didn't cry today, maybe she's becoming more comfortable here," or "I think Judy is getting used to her routine." I desperately wanted her to believe that it was so, and I think she needed to believe it to help her through her own guilt. But this was supposed to be the day that the truth came out, and it wasn't happening.

Later, however, when I was saying goodbye to Brenda, she commented that I seemed quieter than usual and asked if everything was okay. I responded that life—"the Judy thing"—was taking a toll. I have always been generally quiet at social gatherings, but that quick smile I once had was now dimmed considerably. That is not to say that I couldn't—or didn't—laugh. In fact, little two-and-a-half-year-old Julia had me laughing plenty as she danced her ballet for us in the dress-up shoes Great-Aunt Brenda had bought her. (Isn't it amazing how these little ones can bring a smile to our faces and warmth to our hearts, lifting our spirits even when we are so far down?) But when the laughter receded, the dullness returned. It was that dullness that Brenda had noticed.

Finally I had my opening, an opportunity to say the whole, long piece that I had been rehearsing in my head. Instead, I chose to keep it simple. "It's really hard for Judy, being in a place with strangers, away from her home and her family. My mother has convinced herself that Judy has been there for a long time, and David and I have convinced her that Judy is adjusting. For me, it has been the most difficult time in my life." Minimal, yet in its own way, enough. And, though it was only to Brenda, I hoped the message that the situation was far from "fine" would get relayed. I could feel the tears rising, so I turned away to continue my goodbyes. Brenda said, "We'll talk." I didn't answer. I didn't want to have a conversation about this. I wanted to tell my side and be done with it. I just wanted people to know.

When I went to say goodbye to the others, one of them commented, "I didn't get a chance to ask, but I hear that Judy is adjusting—sort of." Maybe it was the addition of the words "sort of" that gave me the courage to speak.

I responded, "Well, she appears to be somewhat adjusting, but it's because she doesn't have a choice." I continued, "She's really not happy." I added my bit about the situation sucking. I kept it short. Again, I didn't go into what it was like to visit. I didn't mention how I had to hold my breath when I got out of the elevator on the second floor until I could tolerate (or somehow ignore) the smell. I didn't elaborate on how Judy sometimes looked so sad and miserable when I arrived for my visit. Adding details required more energy than I had. I generalized and said what I wanted to say about how difficult the situation as a whole was for me and for Judy without getting emotional, and she listened. And that was that. And even though I didn't get to tell everyone, I was glad that I had left there with at least two people knowing. And, again, I hoped the message would get relayed to the others.

Earlier in the evening, my brother Orin, who was spending the weekend at Brenda's in White Plains where we celebrated that year, had mentioned he was planning to visit Judy on Sunday before he went home to Cherry Hill. It would be his first visit since shortly after Judy went in. I wondered what feelings he would come away with, and I was interested to hear what he would say after the visit.

A couple of days afterward, I discovered that my feelings had been relayed, and Carrie called saying that I had seemed to be a bit down at dinner. We had a pretty long talk (probably way overdue), and I calmly explained why I was down—how I felt when I visited Judy, how I felt about TNH, the frustrations I felt each time I visited, and so on. "You know, I say things are okay, but they're really not. It's pretty awful going to TNH even twice a week and seeing so many disabled people. And Judy is one of them."

Carrie replied, "Yes, it has to be hard to see Judy in a place where the people who take care of her don't know her and don't love her."

I also aired my fears for the future. "I don't see an end to this situation until one of us, Judy or myself, dies. And I'm beyond petrified that I could die first and leave her all alone." Carrie was very sympathetic and suggested, not for the first time, that I get some counseling. Looking back now, I was remiss in not taking her advice. At the time I couldn't imagine that it would help me. I thought, *How could anyone understand what I'm going through, even a trained therapist? It would only leave me feeling frustrated and hopeless.*

Journal Entry
November 30, 2005
Yesterday was Judy's three month "anniversary" at TNH. My mother, who lately gets confused about time issues, thinks we are mistaken—it must be longer. If not for the calendar and the verification that it is not

a mistake, I would agree with her completely. Three months can, indeed, seem like a very long time.

Recently, when a friend asked me how things were going with Judy, and I gave my true assessment of the situation, she asked if there was a support group I could join or if, at least, I had any kind of support system. I mentioned David. Throughout the most difficult days of my life, he has remained my rock. He was there for me when my father got sick and ended up in the hospital, never recovering from the operation he had undergone to remove the cancer in his esophagus. David had put Ronen in the car and driven me into Manhattan, then sat double-parked with Ronen for as long as it took so I could say goodbye to my dad. When I returned to the car afterward, he hugged me and said, "Good you went to see him. It was important."

When I decided I wanted to go back to school at Bank Street in Manhattan but wasn't sure I could actually succeed, he was right there, building my confidence. "You can do it. You're smart. You're capable. You'll do great!" And David was never one to say things just to make me feel good. When he said something, I knew he believed it to be true. Then, when the master's program began, and I worried about how I would get there—nervous about driving into the city, apprehensive about taking the train—he drove me. He picked me up at work on Long Island, drove me all the way to Upper Manhattan, hung around until I was finished, and then picked me up and drove me home. He continued to do this until I was comfortable making the trip by myself.

Now, despite our mutual revulsion over TNH, he continues to tell me that we did the right thing. "It was necessary. We had to do it. Your mother is better off, and even Judy is better off. It will be okay. Everything will be okay." And because he says it with such confidence, I have almost no choice but to believe him.

10

Some Sunshine, Some Rain

I took a small parkway on my way to and from Judy. How pretty it was in November, lined with trees showing their rainbows of autumn colors. As I drove, I would come to a rise in the road, and each time I reached the top of this little hill, I was delighted anew by the sight of the first body of water of the trip. My heart skipped a beat at its beauty, and then another beat, with each successive view of the bay, separated only by fields of wild growth now dotted with red, orange, and yellow bushes and the sway of tall beige-pink autumn stalks waving in the breeze. My feelings of wonder and awe were mixed with a hard-to-describe sense of openness, and as I crossed any one of the several small drawbridges on my trip, I would experience a sensation of freedom as my eyes peered out across the water. The beauty of the world is what gave me hope amid all the sadness. David had found a new route to TNH, slightly shorter in mileage as well as in time. But I stuck to my parkway route and my marine view. It helped sustain me. You might say it nourished my spirit.

Driving home after my visit, my mind would often turn to thoughts of Judy in her better days when she laughed more easily in response to stories I would tell her: short tales about our family and friends, about things we were doing; silly things the kids did and silly things David did. Tales that I knew would bring her joy. "Ronen is coming to visit from Boston. Remember when he was little, how he used to sit on your lap, and we'd ride around the apartment? We'd start out in the living room, then go down the hallway and into your room, then out and into Mommy's room. And with all the twists and turns, we had to make sure he didn't fall off!" Or, "David rode his bike to get coffee. He has to have his coffee every morning, you know. Otherwise he gets very grumpy! And nobody wants David to be grumpy!" She would start off by vocalizing what sounded like a protest, as if she were saying, "What? You can't tell that story!" Then she would start laughing loudly, delighting in the memory, bringing a huge smile to my face as well. How I loved telling her stories. How I loved to hear her laugh!

Even in times of despair, there are events that can make us smile. On one of my visits to Judy, I was looking for some Vaseline to put on her dry lips. The aides kept a bin of her personal toiletries (toothbrush and toothpaste, hairbrush, etc.) in a cabinet next to Judy's bed. I didn't find Vaseline, but I did find a large can of shaving cream. I showed it to Judy and asked her why she had shaving cream with her stuff. I was not, of course, expecting an answer, but maybe a laugh, but I got no response. She just looked at me like I was nuts. She clearly had no idea what I was talking about. I explained, "This is shaving cream. Men use it to shave their mustache and beard. You don't have a mustache, and you don't have a beard." I thought I would get at least a smile. Instead, all I got was another blank stare. I briefly thought that maybe they had finger-painted with Judy but discarded that idea because it was very unlikely (as nothing like that seemed to go on there), and why would they put the cream in with her stuff? So I decided that maybe it got there by mistake, and I just forgot about it.

Later on, when we got back from our walk and I put Judy on her bed, I went to cover her a little with the sheet and her leg caught my eye. It was strange looking, so I looked closer. Her leg was shiny. I couldn't figure out what was wrong with her skin, and then I realized they had shaved Judy's legs! It was so sweet! Judy had never had her legs shaved before. In fact, she probably had no idea what they were doing to her. She may even have thought it was some kind of medical procedure. Now, you have to picture Judy's legs. They were the skinniest things ever made. So now they looked like smooth, shiny poles.

I exclaimed, "Now I understand what the shaving cream is for!" Poor Judy still had no idea what that meant, and all I got were more blank stares. "When girls grow up, they shave their legs to get rid of the hair. It makes their legs smooth." I think she thought I had lost my mind. I gave up with my explanations. I remained amazed, however, that someone had noticed the hair on her legs and taken the time to shave them to make her look pretty! How powerful a simple act of kindness and caring can be, lifting us up and giving us a sense of, *It's going to be okay.* How loving. How human.

Before Thanksgiving, sensing that I was depressed, a friend asked me to list the things for which I was thankful. Remembering our good fortune helps us focus on the positives in our lives rather than harp on the difficulties. I replied, "I am thankful for many things, among them family and friends, autumn trees, the full moon, and sunshine." I could also have added things like my work, my education, and much, much more. As I continued my conversation with my friend, I added, "And I am also thankful for Eddie. I am so grateful that he came our way."

Eddie had moved into the extra bedroom in my mother's apartment in exchange for keeping an eye on her. The importance of caring for and honoring the elderly was important in Eddie's culture, and he seemed thrilled to have the opportunity to do what he considered a good deed. Most importantly, my mother really liked him. His English was better than his mother's (whose native language was Chinese), and he conversed more with Mom. Sometimes they drank tea together.

I had begun to see that David's idea of asking Eddie if he would be willing to drive my mother to TNH on Saturdays could work. I realized it would be fine if he waited there and then brought her back to her house. Despite her declining memory and physical strength, my mother was a capable woman. I had to trust that she would figure out how to manage. Sometimes David could even meet her there, and Eddie would still take her home. The first time we tried it, David met Eddie at TNH just to make sure everything went okay. Eddie found something to do while he waited, and when it was time to pick my mother up from her visit, he went upstairs to get her. He could have driven her straight home, but instead he took her to the boardwalk at the beach so she could walk a bit near the ocean. She loved it! He then took her shopping at the Chinese grocery, stopping by his family's home with her to say hello. Although she couldn't remember all the details, she reported to me, "I had a very nice day!"

It's interesting how, though we may hope that our loved ones will always be there in times of need, sometimes we have to turn outside the family for help. Though I'm sure Orin wanted to help more in caring for Judy, it just wasn't feasible. Eddie became an important support for David, Mom, and me.

When Orin did come, it was to benefit Judy. As his visits were occasional, he didn't have a deep understanding of my feelings about the situation. After his second visit, he didn't comment on TNH itself but reported that "Judy seems to be adjusting. She seemed happy enough when I saw her." Judy, in all likelihood, was very happy to see Orin, and he most likely regaled her with his stories that made her laugh a lot. I decided to accept the situation as it was and be content with as many visits as he could arrange.

I started having "okay" days. Not necessarily all good, but on the whole, not bad. A few of my friends asked to come with me on an occasional visit. Fran, a colleague at the day school where we both taught and whom I had known for many years, joined me on multiple occasions, and I found I really enjoyed having someone else with me to experience what I had been talking about. Of course, each friend who came saw it through their own eyes, which may have been very different from what I saw, but it didn't matter. I had someone other than David and my mom to share it with.

Bobby was very talkative on one of Fran's visits, and we had a long conversation about Christmas and what gift he wanted and that he was going to a party. A resident standing next to Bobby overheard and commented that they would be having a party at TNH. Being Jewish, we celebrated Chanukah, and as we left Bobby for our walk, I told

Judy, "Chanukah and Christmas come at the same time this year, so I think they'll have a party for both holidays." Her eyes crinkled and her lower lip came out in a pout. "I want to get a chanukiah that I can put in your room." (A chanukiah is a special menorah used to light the Chanukah candles.) More pouting. My stomach tightened. I thought she might cry. Fran stood, watching and listening. "They don't allow real candles in the rooms, but I can get an electric one." Her expression was still pouty, with more tightening. "They might even light candles here in the rec room." I avoided mentioning my mother. It had been Judy and Mom for so many years. "Just like I used to come one night and light candles with you at home, I'll come to TNH one night and we can light candles together." Her pout disappeared, and a smile took its place. My stomach relaxed, though not completely. I changed the subject, and we continued walking.

Somewhere on our walk, we saw Susie sitting in the hall, and I said hello. She didn't answer, which surprised me because I didn't think she would have forgotten me already from our previous encounter, but I didn't think much more about it. Judy, Fran, and I continued walking for a little bit and then returned to Judy's room, and I put her on her bed. She started kvetching and twisting her head back to seemingly look at the pictures, so I moved some of them so she could see them better. She was still kvetchy. I felt my body tighten and worried that maybe I shouldn't have moved the pictures because, if she was lying on her other side, she wouldn't be able to see any of them. I rearranged a little more, but she was still kvetchy. I had no idea what she wanted, but I kept fiddling with the pictures because that was the direction that she kept twisting her head, and I hoped it would cause her to relax. The tension left my body as Judy's body finally loosened up and she stopped kvetching. Fran and I said goodbye, and Judy seemed okay. In retrospect, I don't think it had anything to do with the pictures. She was simply twisting her body because it was all she could do to show her dissatisfaction with something. Most likely, it was something I said that finally caused her to relax. Either that, or she simply gave up.

On my way out of the elevator in the lobby, we ran into Susie going up. She gave me a big hello, and I realized that the person to whom I had said hello earlier, the one who hadn't responded, wasn't Susie at all! I laughed at myself and said to Fran, "I really have to start talking to these residents more. How can I get to know them otherwise?" Fran agreed, saying that getting to know the people who live here would make this place more bearable for me. I reminded myself of something really important—that when we get to know someone, we stop focusing on the disability and start seeing the person. A good thing to remember!

The following day, it became clear that Judy's shoulder sore was not getting any better, and because of this sore, Judy continued to be kept out of the chair. I had already spoken to the person in charge of wheelchairs about the headpiece needing to be adjusted, and I figured it was taking a while to get it fixed, but I didn't know how much longer this would take, and I didn't want Judy staying on the bed so much. I put in a call to Mary, the "chair lady," who called me back with the message that she would be in the center the coming Saturday. I asked David to speak to her when he was there, and Mary filled him in. Judy's sore was badly infected, and she had developed a fever. She was on an oral antibiotic as well as antibiotic cream. David conveyed my message that we didn't want Judy staying on the bed until the situation improved, which we feared would be a while. Mary told him, "We're looking into redoing the entire chair. In the meantime, we were able to cut out a large piece from the seat cushion, allowing her body to drop down and not rub against the support piece at her shoulder." David also learned that the doctor had been there to see Judy. The area had become irritated because Judy had gained seven pounds and fit differently in the chair now. I didn't think her weight gain should make that big a difference and thought the change was more likely due to the progressive curvature of Judy's spine, but I kept my thoughts to myself. I was quite upset that it took a major infection to get them moving, as I had previously mentioned my concern over the headpiece. David then relayed to me that there was only one person who could design a new headpiece, and she came in only about once a month. *Breathe! Stay calm! David is only the messenger!*

"In the meantime," Mary had continued, "Judy can use the chair with the revised seat cushion until we go through the necessary channels to get the remodel approved." David mentioned that my mother still had an extra chair at home. "By all means, bring it in, and Judy can use that in the meantime." David got the extra chair and brought it to our house for me to take the next time I visited, though it wouldn't be a Saturday, and I would have preferred Mary be there to approve of how Judy was sitting in it. I didn't want any additional problems caused by this chair.

It turned out that the doctor who had visited Judy mentioned that Judy's spine was worsening, confirming my own suspicion. "The doctor would like a surgeon to look at her in six to eight months, as she may need spinal surgery. There is also a possibility that there will come a time when she won't be able to sit in the chair at all." That was, needless to say, very bad news. I was skeptical about whether, at this point in Judy's life, surgery would be beneficial and felt it would more likely cause needless pain and stress. I was glad the doctor was putting off any action for six to eight months. It gave me the opportunity to pretend it wasn't going to happen.

Thinking about these new developments, however, made me reflect on how fragile Judy was and how much I wished I could keep her safe. It brought up a memory from long ago. We were twelve when a fire broke out in the apartment above us. It was during the day, and my father was at work. My mother was out somewhere with Judy, and I was home with my brother David. The smoke filtered down into our kitchen, and David and I evacuated. I was glad Judy wasn't home, and I cried when I remembered that we had left my bird upstairs. David comforted me as we stood outside waiting for the fire trucks, assuring me that Pee Wee would be okay. When the fire was put out, we were able to return to the apartment. The kitchen was a mess, heavy with the smell of smoke, water pouring down from the apartment above into the cabinets and onto the floor. But we, including Pee Wee, were all safe. Messes can be cleaned up. That night Judy and I went to bed as usual. I was awakened in the middle of the night by the sound of crackling, and when I opened my eyes, I saw a wall of fire outside my window. The firefighters had thrown some of the upstairs furniture down into the narrow alleyway onto which my second-floor bedroom window faced. There must have been lingering embers that reignited during the night. It only took a second for the fire to register in my brain, and instinct took over. I jumped out of bed, ran to Judy, lifted her up, and carried her into my parents' room. The fire trucks came, the fire was put out quickly, and once again we were safe. I will always remember, though, the pride I felt that my first reaction, my first thought, was my sister's safety.

Another example of my protective nature had occurred a couple of years earlier. My grandmother was watching Judy and me. We were in my brothers' room—I don't remember why, as they weren't home. Grandma took Judy out of the wheelchair and, holding her, went to sit down. She missed the chair and, with Judy in her arms, fell to the floor. Judy was not in any real danger, but my reaction was to lift her up and run with her to the other side of the large apartment to deposit her in her bed, where she would be safe, before returning to help my grandmother. I could have put Judy on my brother's bed, which would have been quicker, and I doubt she would have fallen off with the two of us still in the room, yet my instinct was to get her to a secure, safe location—in this case, her bed with the railing.

Though others in my family were clearly looking out for the both of us, I felt a closeness to Judy that I don't think anyone else had. I believed it was my job to protect her and keep her from harm. Maybe that's why I felt so guilty about TNH. I hadn't done my job. I hadn't protected her from the need to be placed in a nursing home, I wasn't able to protect her from spinal deterioration, and I couldn't even protect her from things like chair sores.

Journal Entry
December 9, 2005

I've been spending a lot of time contemplating my anguish, and I came up with a theory of why I'm so miserable. My theory is that I somehow like to be miserable. Or perhaps I need to be miserable. Maybe I want people to feel sorry for me or maybe just to pay attention to me. Or maybe, as I wallow in my misery, I am punishing myself for my guilt— guilt for putting Judy in this place, for leaving her after each visit, for not being a better sister in recent years; guilt, right from the beginning, for being the healthy one.

When I was little, I used to have what I call the "Hero Fantasy." I was a kind of superwoman. I would jump into burning buildings and save the people trapped inside. Nothing could hurt me, so I was able to rescue those in need, which made me a hero. People would be in awe of my "wonderfulness." As an adult, looking back, I realize that this fantasy may have had something to do with the fact that even though I was a girl following two older brothers, I probably did not get as much atten- tion as I would have liked. I fault no one and never have. Never, in all my years, did I feel any anger or resentment toward Judy for "stealing" attention from me, nor toward my parents for giving her more. But I think there was a need for recognition—"Here I am! Please see me"—to which the fantasy was my response. So, in my theory, it is this need for recognition that has been causing me to be miserable, as I secretly hope that people will notice me, even if it is to feel sorry.

The other part of my theory—the guilt part—brings me back to that moment with my father when I said I wished I could change places with Judy. He got upset—one of the few times he ever did with me—and responded, "I don't ever want to hear you say that again." In retrospect, it was undoubtedly not the best response he could have given. But even then, at around eight years old, I knew it was out of love for me. He could not bear the thought of losing me, even though it would mean having his other daughter "whole." What he didn't know was that I didn't mean that I would change places with Judy and totally become her. What I had in mind was that I would still be me and I would know all the things

I knew, so that even being in Judy's body, I would somehow be able to overcome the cerebral palsy. Because I had once been able-bodied, I would be capable of teaching myself to walk and talk and do all those things, and then we would both be okay. So, my guilt theory includes not only my being born "typical" and my inability to fix the situation and "make her better" but also the knowledge that, though I was willing to make an exchange, it was not unconditional. Oh, the weight of having a disabled twin!

11

Chairs, Candles, and Change

Judy seemed a lot more comfortable in her new chair (which was really the old chair from home), but it needed some adjustments. Mary and the person in charge of designing the chair modification were due to come to TNH. Even without the modifications, though, Judy sat better in the chair, her body more relaxed and with less twisting and turning. I figured it was because she was no longer rubbing against the headrest, and her shoulder wound was finally healing. I realized she must have been in a lot of pain from it, and that was creating some of her distress when I visited. I also thought that she liked having Fran visit with me, even though she hadn't known Fran before. She became quite "talkative," laughing and making her characteristic happy sounds, more like her old self. One afternoon, as she came out of the dining room, I was standing in the hall nearby looking at Susie's photo album of her twin sister's wedding. Susie had caught me and Fran waiting in the hall and brought the album from her room to show us. Judy started laughing when she saw us standing there looking at the pictures. I remember what a nice feeling it was for me, hearing Judy's spontaneous laughter.

I suppose that I, though still finding the smells repulsive, was also more relaxed as I was getting used to the residents at TNH. I hadn't seen Bobby on my prior visit, and I found that I missed him! I looked for him on this visit and again didn't see him until he called out to me from his room—he was lying in bed because his chair needed to be repaired. He asked me the usual, "Do you have any questions for me?"

I complied, "Bobby, is anything new going on?"

"I'm going home for Christmas!" Fran and I both smiled in response to his excitement. All in all, things were still looking up, and I was feeling more hopeful. Though I didn't always feel like making the trip to TNH after work, and I still worried about what time I should go and whether I would have to feed Judy, I no longer dreaded the visits and actually even looked forward to seeing the people I now knew. It had taken me time to feel comfortable in this new situation.

Judy's shoulder was definitely healing. There was a new sore beginning, though, on her left hip where her bone protruded and her thin skin had started to tear. The plan was to make a new mold for Judy's regular chair. In the meantime, they once again wanted Judy in the chair as little as possible and had given her a geri chair. Made for geriatrics, a geri chair is like a recliner on wheels. It allowed Judy to lie down with her back elevated. I remembered seeing a woman being wheeled around on one of those chairs on my very first visit to TNH, when it was still owned by UCP. It looked more like a bed on wheels than a chair, and I had been perversely pleased to see that there was someone worse off than Judy. Ironically, it was now Judy who needed one. When I asked Judy about being in that kind of chair, she indicated that they had already been using it with her whenever they got her off the bed. I was glad they were getting Judy out of bed but didn't like that she was unable to use a wheelchair, as that meant she was becoming even more disabled.

Thinking about this, I had a flashback to younger days when Judy didn't need the headrest and was able to hold her head up, though her body slouched a little to one side. My grandfather was still alive then. Whenever he saw Judy, he would approach her in her chair, put out his hand, and wait for Judy to give him hers. She would smile and slowly, with great effort, lift a hand about two or three inches off her lap to meet his outstretched palm. What a proud accomplishment that always was. Over the years, as her muscles tightened, her ability to control any movement lessened, and now here we were, at a point where even sitting in the chair presented problems. Needless to say, I wasn't happy about the entire situation, but I was learning to accept that this was the way it was, that there are things over which we just have no control, and that acceptance can be a real stress reducer. I also realized that Judy's care had been about as good as it could have been and, even though the aides were not there to check on her every minute, and she may have sometimes sat in a wet or dirty diaper longer than I would have liked, they did seem to be on top of the wound situation, and that was very important.

In my efforts to help Judy feel more at home, I started focusing on how and when to light Chanukah candles and what kind of chanukiah to get. I wanted to be with Judy to light the first candle, but the first night coincided with a Chanukah party at my nephew's home in Pennsylvania. I thought maybe David and I would leave the party earlier than originally planned so we could visit Judy afterward. I felt it was important to try to keep alive as much of the family home traditions as possible. Mom had always lit candles with Judy, and my family and I would go to her apartment once during the week to light with them. Since Mom wasn't going to be at TNH to light candles with Judy this year, and live candles wouldn't be permitted, I came up with a plan: we'd use an electric chanukiah and turn on bulbs each night while saying the blessings. Reality check: *I do not want to go there every night.* Immediate revision: *It will be okay to "light the candles" three or four times during the eight days.* Seemed reasonable.

We bought the chanukiah and took it to TNH the day before Chanukah. So far, so good! I really wanted to light the first candle with her, but the logistics of driving to Pennsylvania and back just wouldn't allow for it. *I'll go in the morning before we leave for my nephew's and light the chanukiah with her then. Technically, not kosher, but sometimes the rules need to be bent. I'll leave a note there for the aides explaining that they can pull the plug each night when Judy goes to sleep, and the next night around five o'clock they can plug it in and turn on the next bulb.* That allowed me the opportunity to begin the candle-lighting process and the luxury of not going every day. I woke up that morning all set to go with my plan. I left the house and headed for TNH. Problem: I couldn't see fifty feet in front of me because of the fog. I turned around and returned home. *Okay, so it's not the end of the world that I won't light the first candle with her. After all, I had told Judy that I would* try *to come.* New revision: *I'll call TNH at around five thirty and ask them to turn on the appropriate bulbs of the chanukiah and to explain to Judy that I couldn't come but that I would try to come the next afternoon.* Suddenly, it wasn't so important to light that first candle with Judy. Interesting how what's important can change so quickly and what seems like a huge hurdle suddenly can become insignificant. In the end, I did "light" candles with Judy twice during the week, and before I knew it, Chanukah was over.

One day shortly afterward, upon my arrival for a visit, Judy was lying on her bed completely twisted—half on her back, half on her side, her neck stretched with her head back, her feet bent at the knees in the most awkward position. She was making a low complaining noise. Her TV and radio were off, but Erika's TV was on loud enough for both of them. When I came in and said hello, she gave me a pained look that said how uncomfortable she was. I started to straighten her out and saw that her leg had locked in an awkward position. It was totally rigid, as if it had cramped up, and I couldn't massage it out. I turned Judy onto her side and, thankfully, her leg automatically relaxed, and her face appeared more comfortable. We went on with our usual visiting talk, listened to Chanukah songs on one of the new CDs that I'd bought her for the holiday, then continued talking. About forty minutes after my arrival, Erika's aide came in to get her up from her nap. I realized that if I had not been there, Judy would have been lying in her uncomfortable position for at least an additional forty minutes—and that's if the aide noticed her! I had no idea how long she had already been like that. At one time, not long before, I would have been really upset at this. I'm not sure that it's a good thing, but that day I wasn't upset at all. It was reality. It was the way things were. Very often when I walked in and Judy was on the bed, her head was twisted back. This was the first time her leg was locked when I arrived, but it probably wasn't the only time it had happened, and I felt sadly sure it wouldn't be the last. *I can mention it to the head nurse and ask that someone check on her more frequently, but other than that, there's not much I can do.* The only other thing would be for me to go there every day and check for myself. Since I wasn't able to do that, I learned to accept the situation. I wasn't happy that she was uncomfortable, but neither was I in distress or guilt-ridden over it. In fact, I surprisingly felt no guilt. Just numb acceptance.

Change is a part of life. I know that. Not just plans change, life itself changes. Ideas, events, feelings don't even *rarely* stay the same forever. They *never* stay the same. Sometimes things get better, sometimes they get worse, but they never stay the same. Sometimes it takes longer, sometimes not long at all. Situations may remain, but the emotions or surrounding events change, and that makes the wholeness of it change. So even when we are at our deepest low and think that things will remain that way forever, there is always change. Sometimes our lows go even lower, we hope they go higher, but they never stay the same.

So things changed. Undoubtedly, they would change again. Maybe the situation, maybe the emotions, maybe the surrounding details. There were ups and there were downs, but things did not stay the same. It worried me, and I tried so hard not to get ahead of myself. For although I couldn't foresee all the changes that would occur, I could foresee one change—that of the inevitable passing of my mother. At some point, this would happen, and I would once again fall into the abyss. But even when that ultimately happened, things would inevitably change once more. And with the prospect of change came the hope of things getting better. I had once feared that Judy's stay at TNH would not get any better. I couldn't imagine it. I was near the bottom, in what I thought was the darkest part of the tunnel, and I was unable to see that proverbial light. True, Judy was currently still at TNH. But the wholeness of the situation had changed, and for the time being, even with the guilt I still felt about putting her there, the recent change was good.

*

Over a week passed until my next visit—the longest I'd ever gone. I had gotten sick with a really bad cold and didn't want to share it with Judy. I didn't know if it made a difference to her or not that I hadn't been there. I didn't know if she knew how many days passed and whether she was wondering where I was. On the day when I resumed my visits, Judy's aide came in to change her diaper and put her in the chair. She asked me if I would be staying for dinner. I said no. I was really tired, still recuperating from being sick, and felt bad about not staying longer but not bad enough to feed her. I didn't know who was more unhappy about that—Judy or the aide!

In the meantime, the aide put Judy in the geri chair, and we went for a hall walk. That was what we had started doing when the weather got too cold to walk outside, and I found it wasn't as bad as I had thought it would be—a little tedious going up and down the corridors, but at least we were moving. On our way down the hall, we met Olivia, another visitor I had spoken to before, and stopped to say hello. "How are things going?" she asked. "Is Judy happy here?"

I didn't know what to say, and I didn't want Judy to hear me say it, so from behind her, I kind of made a face that said *no, not really*, and aloud said, "She seems to be content. At least I assume so because she doesn't cry." I turned to look at Judy and, for some reason, she started laughing.

Olivia quietly said, "Judy does cry—often." I didn't know if Judy heard that because she kept on laughing, but I heard it, and it was like a kick in the heart. Remember that heart that had pieces being chipped away? I thought I had reached the point where no more damage could be done. I was wrong. I tried to find out if there was a pattern to the crying, like a particular time of day or when she was on the bed or in the chair. Olivia didn't know, except that she only came in the evenings and thought it was after supper. "Maybe Judy is tired," she suggested. I said that she probably starts out complaining and then, when no one comes, she cries. I was unhappy to hear Olivia's "report" and at first thought, *Olivia should keep those things to herself. They're upsetting, and what can I do about it?* Then I realized that, if other people didn't tell me what was going on, I would never know. Not knowing can *seem* like a good thing. As they say, ignorance is bliss, but not knowing is not really good.

A little while later, after Judy and I had left Olivia and were continuing our walk, I asked Judy about it. I was afraid that I would upset her, but I had to ask. "Jude, do you cry sometimes when I'm not here? You know, it's okay to cry if you need someone and they don't come. Is that why you cry? Because you want someone to come?" She opened and closed her mouth in her way that indicated, "Yes. That's why I cry." I didn't know if it was true, or if she just said it. I didn't know how often she cried. I didn't know if it was because she didn't like what was on TV or if she was uncomfortable in her bed, if she was sad, or if she was lonely, or if she cried for any other number of reasons. I imagined that, at any given time, it could have been any one of those.

It was time for me to leave, and as I got ready to go, I felt my muscles tensing, my throat constricting, and my head starting to throb. I sat down next to Judy and looked her in the eyes. "When I come, I can only stay for a little while because I want you to eat in the dining room. I get stressed when I feed you because I don't think I'm doing a good job." You should have heard me trying to explain to her what "stressed" means. Then I went on about how it all makes me feel guilty, and I had to explain what "guilty" means. By the end of it all, Judy was twisting her head toward the door, indicating she wanted to go into the dining room for dinner. I brought her in and she relaxed—probably happy that my babbling had finally come to an end. I, on the other hand, felt sad. And with this emotion, I began and ended my journey home.

Journal Entry
January 12, 2006

During my ride down to TNH, I wondered how much longer I would be able to do this. Am I going to last a lifetime? Because that's how much time will be needed. I didn't know. On the way home, I could only think about Judy's life and the what-ifs. What if something happens to me? What if Judy lives longer than I do? What if I get too old to visit? What if I get too old to remember to visit? What if there is no one left to visit Judy? What if? What if? I know I'm not supposed to worry about things that aren't in my control, and I do think I've gotten better about not feeling so guilty, but I still worry. When I was pregnant with my kids, I wanted to be able to remove them from my belly—just for a moment—to ensure that everything was okay, and then put them back again to continue to grow. Now I just want someone to guarantee me that everything will be okay with Judy. Then I will be okay too. Just someone promise me that. Judy will always have someone. She will never be alone. That's all I ask, just for someone to give me that assurance.

I have a new fantasy now, that Judy is living with me and there is someone to take care of her all the time. This person bathes her and feeds her and talks to her and exercises her arms and legs and takes her for walks. This person makes sure that she is listening to the music and watching the TV shows that she likes. This person spends time with her so that she is not always by herself. And then, when I come home from work, I am near her and can talk to her when I want and sit with her when I want and for as long as I want, and I can go into another room when I want and come back and say hello when I want. And I don't have to worry about visiting. I don't have to worry about whether someone is watching to make sure that she's comfortable on her bed or that she has someone to feed her. And I don't have to deal with Martha, yelling and cursing in the hall, or Erika's TV being too loud, or the foul smell of the place. And I don't have to worry about going on vacation and leaving her without me; I'll know that she is happy and well cared for because the person taking care of her will love her. And I don't ever have to worry that she'll be alone. I will know that she is happy and that she will always be happy. That is how I wish things could be. That is my fantasy.

But I know it can't be like that.

But I wish it could.

But I know it can't.

And that makes me sad, sad that I can't be a better sister and make that wish come true.

12
Emotional Mayhem

Almost six months had passed since Judy arrived at TNH. I felt that six months wasn't really a long time in the grand scheme of things, yet it felt like a lifetime ago that this had all begun. And I worried about the future. That much hadn't changed.

On my way home with Fran after one of our visits, we spoke about the purpose of life for Judy and for many of the people at TNH. The topic was not new to me. I had wrestled with it for many years, wondering about Judy's quality of life and trying to imagine what life would have been like without her. My answer never varied. Though there were so many things that Judy couldn't do, she was able to laugh and to love, and that gave her life all the quality that was needed. I never faltered from being very grateful that Judy was my sister and that my parents had not put her into a home from the beginning. I could not imagine life without her. Yet as I grew, I had questioned more and more the *reason* for her existence as it was. I needed to understand why people with disabilities are born into this world, why life isn't simple. I tried to reason that Judy, being who she was, had somehow made me a better person. I really wanted to believe that. And though Judy had a profound influence on the person I became, I didn't take that influence and do any good for the world or even for the Judys of the world. I had, at one time, thought of becoming a physical therapist working with disabled children, but I did not ultimately choose that profession. I had thought of going into special education and working with severely disabled children, but a visit to a school for children with special needs showed me that it upset me too much. So what was the reason Judy was born as she was? I never could come up with an answer to that question and wondered whether there even is a reason. Could it be that Judy and all the others at TNH and elsewhere in this world are who and how they are simply because that's what happens in life? Can it be that there is no spiritual reason why they are who they are any more than there's a reason why I am who I am or you are who you are?

The Judys of the world, though unable to make a contribution to society, unable even to survive on their own, do bring joy into their loved ones' hearts. They make us smile and give us love, and we make them smile and return that love, but I now knew that there comes a time when that happy existence is threatened. When that time comes, how do we let them go on in a life that, to us, seems unbearably diffi-cult? Judy was happy throughout most of her years at home, enjoying being with family, watching her TV shows, and listening to her music, but what joy was she getting at TNH? Having a visitor once or twice a week in what was otherwise a long, drawn-out wait for just those moments? I wondered if it was worth it.

Even before she went to TNH, fearing what was in store, I prayed for some divine intervention to take Judy out of what I thought of as her approaching misery. A part of me had always believed in eutha-nasia, and I had speculated on whether or not I would want that for Judy. I certainly would never have wanted to be the one taking the action. The thought stayed with me, though, for quite some time. At one point, I even considered contacting Dr. Jack Kevorkian, the doctor who helped people die, though I knew he would have never even taken my case, if for no other reason than Judy was not capable of giving her consent, nor was she terminally ill. I also knew that even if I had been able to convince myself that ending Judy's life was the right thing to do, I would never have been able to go through with it. I could not have taken *any* life, certainly not the life of someone I loved so much. So I prayed for answers.

Now that Judy was living in TNH, my prayers continued, but I wondered if I was making them for selfish reasons. Were my current prayers to end what I saw as Judy's suffering based on my desire to end *her* misery, or were they based on me wanting to end *mine*? Most of us would never want to make our lives easier at the expense of someone else, and I didn't want to think that I could be such a person, but it is also unbearable to think of someone we love being in great pain, especially when there is no hope for recovery. As Judy continued her life at TNH, my inner turmoil over her current existence remained, and it was agonizing. I was conflicted over the thought that my desire to end Judy's suffering could be founded on selfishness.

And then, suddenly, in the reality of TNH, the bottom dropped out. Judy was brought to the hospital with what the doctors called an asthma attack. Even though she did not have a long history of asthma, her spine had started to curve more as she aged, and evidently this was compromising her lungs and causing her to wheeze every so often. This trip to the hospital was actually the second time the staff at TNH had called for an ambulance. That first time, I'd had to struggle hard to hold back my tears when I arrived at the emergency room and found Judy, her mouth and nose covered with an oxygen mask, fear emanating from her wide-open eyes. Her breathing seemed even, and I wondered why they had brought her there. The doctors were unsure whether she should be admitted, and I was opposed to it. I didn't believe she was in any real danger and sensed that the hospital was not a good place for her. I'm not sure how I did it, but I convinced them to release her and send her back to TNH. Maybe it was because it was a small hospital and they didn't really know how to treat her. I didn't care. I only knew that she didn't have to stay there, and that's all that mattered to me. And in fact, she was breathing fine when she got back to TNH, and the problem didn't recur for some time.

That was before, however. This time, Judy was definitely in respiratory distress when she arrived at the emergency room, where she spent the next day and a half before being admitted. She had a fever of 103 and continued to have difficulty breathing. One of the doctors reported to me that if Judy hadn't had a DNR (do-not-resuscitate order), she would have been put on a ventilator—and she might never have been free of the device. I couldn't help feeling that I had done something right, getting the DNR. How awful it would have been for Judy to have to live the rest of her life hooked up to a machine, unable even to breathe on her own, taking away one of the few independent acts she had.

Judy was in a regular hospital room for three and a half days receiving various medications to help her breathe and reduce her fever, and then, during one of my visits, I noticed her having a seizure. She had never in her life had one, but I recognized the signs: her eyes rolled back in her head, her head rigid, and her body shaking slightly. I notified the nurse. A short time later, Judy was taken to the CCU (cardiac care unit).

Her fever, which had previously dropped, was back up to 103. Her skin was ashen, her face drawn, and heavy bags lay under her eyes. That first seizure lasted a seemingly never-ending three hours. It was mostly mild, her eyes rolled up, her throat constricted, and her left hand rigid, with occasional spikes of heavier shaking. I felt her exhaustion. I wished it would just stop and she would go to sleep. I was wishing for regular sleep, but part of me wondered if permanent sleep might not be so bad. I had always hoped that when she died, it would be peaceful. This was far from peaceful. Watching Judy seize was only second to watching her fight for every breath. But all that was nothing compared to the inner fight I was having about wishing it would all just end.

The seizure finally stopped and, with her face relaxed, she looked peaceful in her sleep. She had another brief seizure and then went back to sleep. Dr. S came in about an hour later, and we talked a bit about Judy's prognosis. He couldn't say for sure. Her wheezing had improved. It was up to the pulmonologist to decide whether and when to remove the face mask that was providing her with oxygen. "If we find a cause for the seizures, we may be able to find a cure. We also don't yet know what is causing the fever."

The biggest issue was feeding—the swallow evaluation that had been done several days earlier had come back with bad results. It advised that she no longer get nourishment by eating, and that a feeding tube be inserted directly into her stomach. The doctor then brought up the possibility of hospice—palliative care with no medication or treatment that could prolong life, only that which would alleviate her pain. Although I had been having inner conflicts about the quality of Judy's life and had sometimes wished it all would end, denying her treatment felt as if I would purposefully be ending her life. That felt wrong because I didn't think Judy was dying. And I didn't understand that, by recommending hospice, the doctors believed that she was. I may have been engaged in selective hearing, my mind choosing to hear only parts of what I was being told because the other parts were too painful to acknowledge. I thought I knew what I wanted and, as Judy's legal guardian, I could have made the decision on my own, but I found myself suddenly hesitant about the finality of it all and felt I needed to involve the family.

When Judy was taken for a CT scan to see if a cause could be found for the seizures, I went home to relay the recent events to my mother, my brothers, and any friends who had called. I found myself not minding repeating my story over and over again, as it seemed to help me absorb the reality and give me the opportunity to integrate all that had happened.

David agreed that my mother and brothers should be a part of the decision of whether or not to put Judy on hospice. He wanted the responsibility to be shared and not to fall solely on my shoulders. My mother, of course, was upset that Judy had needed to be hospitalized, but it wasn't the first time that had happened. Judy had had issues with wheezing before, and one of her more attentive home attendants would get nervous every time it happened and had twice called 911. Judy had been taken by ambulance to the local hospital. I had been against this because I didn't think the wheezing was so bad, and I didn't think the doctors knew how to properly treat Judy. My mother had been allowed to ride with her in the ambulance, though, and at least I felt comforted that Judy wasn't afraid. Her stay in the hospital was never more than a few hours.

This time was different, of course, and my mother was quite concerned, yet she didn't think that hospice was necessary—she, too, did not believe Judy was dying—and wasn't sure about the feeding tube. My brothers, as I expected, said they would go along with whatever our mother and I decided. They were very supportive, and neither one wanted Judy to suffer. The question remained: Was she sufficiently aware of what was happening to *be* suffering, and would she be suffering if she were to recover from the seizures and returned to TNH?

So there I was, no clearer about what to do—not wanting to be a part of ending Judy's life and yet wishing that her suffering would end. All I could think about was, *When will this ordeal be over?* When the doctors came in to see Judy, my questions all related to taking her off support, such as, "How long do you think she will live?" and, "Will she die peacefully?" I wondered what they thought of me. *Only awful people don't want their loved ones to get better. Only awful people hope that each breath will be the last.* I imagined that they saw me as being in a rush for it to happen. And in a way, I was. I was in a rush to end what I saw as her misery. But I also kept wondering, *Is it really misery? What exactly is the depth of her suffering? At what point is it okay to choose to let someone die?*

David brought my mom to the hospital to see Judy and speak to Dr. S. I was happy to relinquish decision-making to her. As long as she agreed with me on the DNR issue—which she did—and on the feeding tube issue (no tube), I was okay. I backed down a bit on the idea of withdrawing treatment altogether, though I was still in favor of applying for hospice care. My impression from Dr. S was that Judy was not going to get better. Presented with that reality, I found myself in conflict. The idea of Judy never recovering from the seizures and continuing to suffer from an inability to breathe freely was too hard for me to accept, and I consoled myself by thinking, *Even doctors can't see the future.*

Judy's illness was well timed in terms of my work. I was on midwinter break. I sat with her all day, every day. I actually found it easy sitting there while she was "sleeping," a euphemism for her coma-like state. I didn't have to tend to her. I just sat nearby or gently rubbed her arm or head. The nurse's aide commented on what a good sister I was. I didn't feel like a good sister. *What am I doing for Judy besides wishing she would leave us? I certainly wasn't a very good sister during the years when I was raising my own children and left Judy's care completely up to my mother and the home attendants. Visiting Judy more often at home and spending time with her when I had other things going on in my life—that would have been a good sister. As it happened, I ultimately failed her as a sister. The little that I do now doesn't even count. Too little, too late!* Guilt had certainly skewed my thinking.

When I got back to the CCU the following day, Mike, Judy's wonderful CCU nurse, mentioned that he had noticed some improvement. Judy's breathing had become easier, and her seizures were shorter. I, too, noticed breathing improvement, but I wasn't as sure about the seizures. I still hadn't seen her conscious. Mike said she opened her eyes twice and looked at him and made a noise. I hadn't seen anything like that and, until I did, I couldn't think she was getting better. I decided to permit nourishment through a tube that was already placed in her mouth for medication. I decided I wouldn't have it removed until she either got better or we decided to go to hospice.

When I asked about that issue, Dr. S couldn't rule out the possibility of her getting better—but why would hospice accept her if that were the case? The doctor said I couldn't refuse feeding her, and yet they asked my permission to give her nourishment through the tube, so I was confused. I asked lots of questions, but I must not have been asking the right ones because I was very unclear about my options and their consequences, so I remained unsure of what to do. In the state Judy was in, I had no problem putting her on hospice. But Mike kept saying she was getting better. *If she gets better, do I have the right to do that? And why would hospice accept her if she can get better?* I was spinning in circles.

Meanwhile, the seizures, albeit shorter than the initial one, continued. Her temperature dropped to 101.9, and the results of the CT scan weren't back yet. She had a rash on her face from the oxygen mask and a sore on top of her ears from the elastic. Mike loosened the band and pulled the mask away from her face a little. He said he would ask about reducing the oxygen and possibly removing the mask altogether. This was the kind of thing that upset me so much because I knew that if it did bother Judy, she couldn't tell us. She couldn't ask for cream or for someone to move the elastic to a different spot. She certainly couldn't move it herself. These types of problems caused so much of my distress because they exemplified her helplessness.

Mike returned and took off the face mask, replacing it with nasal oxygen, and suctioned the "gook" out of her mouth. Judy appeared to be sleeping and looked much better. I was still waiting for her to wake up. Mike had made a reasonable point when he said that she wasn't waking because of all the medication she was receiving. He also explained about the stomach feeding tube, called a gastronomy (G) tube. Though it required surgery, it would just be a small slit in the skin near her belly, and the tube would get inserted directly into the stomach. He said it didn't prevent the person from eating regular food (of course that would depend on Judy's swallow evaluations), only ensured that the person would be fully nourished. "She'll probably be healthier than she was before." *He sure is an optimist,* I thought, *and he clearly believes that life, every life, is worth saving.*

My latest question: *What are the implications of having a tube inserted in the stomach in regard to hospice?* My understanding at the time was that she wouldn't be a candidate for hospice as long as she had the tube. But, once in, could I have it removed? Wouldn't that be like killing her? How could that be allowed?

I wasn't ready to make any decisions as long as Judy was unconscious—especially any irreversible decisions. If Judy were never to wake up, it would be an easy decision. If Judy did awaken, it would be more complicated. I started wondering if Judy's breathing problems were partially due to her aspirating while eating and, if she no longer ate through her mouth, the breathing problems might cease. There was another probable cause of the wheezing, though. The increasing curvature of her spine was pressing against her lungs. This was never going to go away, so the chances were that even if this episode were to clear up, it would in all likelihood recur. I felt foolish remembering that I had hoped that Judy might one day live in an IRA. Just another one of my wild fantasies that could never be realized.

In attempting to come to a decision, my family members and I had all asked ourselves, *What would Judy want? Would she want the feeding tube? Would she choose hospice?* None of us had an answer, but I believed that if you simply asked her if she wanted to go back to TNH, she would have quickly said, "No. I want to go home."

I continued to wait for Judy to wake up. In the meantime, I started taking detailed notes:

2:00 another seizure, short—basically eyelid flutterings that last between about 20–30 seconds; back to sleep; 2:39 same as before. . . . My notations continued throughout the afternoon into the evening, detailing more seizures—some one minute in length, some several minutes, but no really long ones. As long as the seizures persisted, I didn't feel it was enough of an improvement, and the only area that had shown any real progress was her breathing, which was the reason she'd been brought to the hospital to begin with. She was still being fed through the orogastric (OG) tube they had going through her mouth—it was a twenty-four-hour process. I knew that when she woke up, we'd have to consider the stomach tube because having a tube going through her mouth down to her stomach would undoubtedly be uncomfortable.

The next day, Judy *looked* like she was awake and more alert, but her eyes, while open, were floating around over to the right, then to the center, then back to the right. She made no sign that she was in distress, so I guessed she was okay. In retrospect, I don't think her mind was fully functioning, though she did respond to my voice and touch by attempting to look at me. She brought her mouth to a *no* position, but I wasn't sure if that was an expression of dissatisfaction or simply a reflex. Her eyes kept closing as if she wanted to sleep, but her eye movements were keeping her awake. Every minute or so, her eyes opened wide for a few seconds. There was no twitching, and her eyes weren't rolling up into her head, yet I wondered if the fluttering movements were another kind of seizure. Her hands and arms were both swollen, evidently due to the fluids she was receiving intravenously. They removed the IV from her left hand (which was more swollen) and started using the right hand IV that was already in place. Her right hand wasn't as badly swollen but was more black-and-blue. When they removed the IV from her left hand, it started oozing fluid from the IV hole. She still had a fever, and they put on the cooling blanket, which they had used previously.

The neurologist came in to report to me early that afternoon. "The brain scan didn't show anything—no bleeds, no masses. The cause of the seizures is seen as medication related, most likely the anti-wheezing medicine." *Was that not just as I had feared when I argued for not calling 911 and sending her to the hospital every time she had a wheezing attack back at home? Was I not correct in knowing that the doctors would be ill-equipped to treat her because they probably had very little experience with someone like Judy? Even I, however, never expected that it would result in making her so much worse!* "The medication seen to be causing the seizures was stopped, and they started her on another, but there is a question about possible residual effects." I could have been angry, but I wasn't. I was simply sad. I didn't blame anyone. I just believed that the doctors had never had a patient like Judy, and they were scrambling in the dark. The neurologist also said it was normal for her to be "dopey" now, and it was common for the dopiness to last several days to a week. He said the seizures may or may not stop altogether. "Sometimes the *electrical disturbance* can continue permanently." He noted that Judy reacted to pain by flinching, but there was no way of knowing if she was cognizant of the feeling or of her reaction. They were planning to do an EEG to see if any seizures were going on in the brain that weren't visible to us. Everything was complicated by the fact that her brain wasn't normal to begin with.

Later in the afternoon, Judy started wheezing again, but she wasn't fighting for every breath, so I was more relaxed. I took advantage of this period of relative calm to have a brief conversation with Dr. S:

Me: Do you know what is causing the fever?

Dr. S: No.

Me: What qualifies Judy for hospice?

Dr. S: The desire of the proxy [me] to discontinue treatment.

Me: How does the feeding tube affect her eligibility?

Dr. S: If a feeding tube is inserted, nourishment would continue, even on hospice.

Me: Would Judy be eligible for hospice while she is in CCU?

Dr. S: No, Judy would have to leave the CCU.

Me: Is there any pain involved after insertion of the tube?

Dr. S: No.

Me: Is the feeding continuous?

Dr. S: Feeding takes place overnight, usually eight p.m. to eight a.m.

Me: How does it affect her getting around in her wheelchair?

Dr. S: It won't.

and finally,

Me: Do you think there is permanent brain damage?

Dr. S: I can't answer that. I don't know.

Dr. S noted that there had been improvements: Though Judy was still wheezing, it was less severe; there was minor seizure activity, also less severe; and her fever was down. She seemed to be stabilizing. He indicated that if the seizures stopped and her fever remained down, they would do another swallow evaluation. If she continued in and out of alertness with on-and-off seizures and continued wheezing, a decision would have to be made whether to give it more time or to apply for hospice. In the doctor's words, Judy seemed to be "on the right track but on a very slow train."

Journal Entry
February 22, 2006

I am in such a state of conflict. Part of me is fearful that Judy will get better and then she (we?) will have to go through her needing to be hospitalized all over again another day. And though I do not want to go through this again for my sake, it is truly Judy I worry about. I do not want her to ever go through this again. Being hospitalized is so much of what I worry about—not only her being in pain but her fear. The look of panic on her face when the nurses tried to put the IV in her arm. The anguish that is so apparent when she begins to cry. The helplessness, both on my part and hers, to get us out of this situation. It's unbearable. Yet she does not appear to be in physical pain, as I imagine people are when they are dying from, say, cancer. So how can I be praying for death? Only a heartless person would do that.

I asked a rabbi friend for guidance. He spoke to my need for a reason that Judy was born the way she was. He spoke to my acute sense of guilt. And he spoke to my confusion as to what I should do. In his words,

"I can't believe that a merciful God would have sent, planned, or done this to your sister. . . . I myself believe that there is no rhyme or reason why bad things happen to good people. Accidents at birth or violence during life take place randomly.

"God or fate has played a terrible trick on your family, and you have done more than most people could or would have done. This is not your fault. From what I know, you can be proud of what you are doing and have done."

Powerful words of support: "This is not your fault." As rational and logical it is to think that none of what has happened has been my fault, the guilt that I have felt my entire life and that still continues has permeated my being.

In response to my question about withholding medication and nutrition, the rabbi went on to say:

"Judaism teaches us that we must prolong life (regardless of its quality), but that we do not prolong death. That is to say, that while we may never do anything to actively end a life, we are not obligated to take

heroic measures to prolong life when a person is at the stage of actually dying.

"Most Jewish opinions hold that while we may withhold machines and medication that keep the person alive, we do not withhold food and water. There is a minority view that sees hydration and nutrition at the end stage as medication, and therefore even those may be withheld."

He advised me to speak to Judy's doctor for guidance about the stomach tube and added that if the doctor and I felt it in Judy's best interest not to continue the feedings,

". . . you could proceed with withdrawing nutrition and hydration and know that significant rabbis would support your decision."

Though he, of course, could not tell me what I should do, I find the rabbi's words to be supportive, and I feel that whatever decision I ultimately make will be the right one for Judy, myself, and the rest of my family. The decision itself, however, remains a difficult one.

So I ask myself, What is it that I want? Do I want Judy to get better? I can't give myself a straight answer. If Judy gets better and ends up getting out of the hospital, I imagine that I'll feel like I was given the chance to end it all and I didn't take it. The door was open, and I couldn't walk through it. That frightens me because, while I had been so worried that Judy might outlive me and one day be alone in the world, I now worry that the day may come when we find ourselves once again in this situation, and I will have caused Judy needless suffering. The thing is, a part of me does want her to get better. A part of me wants life to go back to what it was before she went into the hospital (ironically, the TNH life that I hated so much). But then I ask myself, What exactly would she be getting better for? To wait until that next occurrence? To live unhappily in TNH in the meantime? So I want her to get better, but I also don't want her to get better. I want her to die is what I want! There, I said it. How awful is that? I want my sister to die. I just don't want to be the one causing it.

13
The Storm Abates

Over the next two days, Judy made further improvements. Her breathing was easier, and they reduced her oxygen level. The IV was back in her left hand, which was still swollen but not as bad as before. They increased the amount of food she was getting through the tube, so I supposed that was a good thing. I thought that even if a person didn't eat through their mouth, their tongue and lips must need to get some moisture every now and then. Her lips looked dry, with caked-on "gook" that came up after the nebulizer treatments. Her fever was down with the help of the cooling blanket. Her eyes didn't float as much in her head. Instead, they frequently looked up to her right, as if she were trying to see something just outside her line of vision. It was difficult to tell whether it was that, or if the eye movements were small seizures. She did not look at me when I called her name. I put myself in her line of vision, and I couldn't tell for sure if she saw me, but I thought maybe yes. I thought she heard my voice and was responding with facial expressions, but it was still hard to tell for sure.

She started making some vocalizations. They appeared voluntary and sounded like grunting, expressing discomfort. Periodically her face scrunched up, and her lower lip stuck out as if she were going to cry, but up to that point she hadn't. My assessment was that she was aware and was tolerating the situation. At one point her feeding machine started beeping—this happened occasionally—and an aide came in to fix it. She shut off the machine for a few seconds, and

Judy started to yell. She may have been yelling at the aide for shutting down the machine, her way of saying, "Hey, you're not supposed to do that!" The yell, however, sounded like she was in pain. It seemed as if Judy could feel a difference in her stomach and that maybe when the machine shut off, the tube moved, and it hurt. Whatever it was, it was clear that Judy was responding to what was going on.

At that point, Judy was getting an anticonvulsant through her feeding tube. She was also getting medication to protect her stomach against ulcers. She was definitely on the road to recovery, but she wasn't there yet. I started noticing more small vocalizations and, at the same time, a left pinky twitch. Another form of seizure?

During one visit, all of a sudden, in the midst of nothing in particular going on, she started yelling, like she was going to cry. It was different from when she yelled her disapproval over a story being told to her, or when she yelled at something that happened on TV. It was more of a sound of anguish, on the verge of an all-out cry. I was able to calm her down by gently rubbing her head, but I didn't know what got her started. I thought she might have been in pain, but I couldn't find out what was bothering her. She was definitely distressed about something, and it occurred to me that maybe, as she was recovering, she was starting to become aware of what was going on, and her outburst had been due to fear. Whether it was pain or fear, it tore me up inside.

As time went on, I was finally able to ask her some questions and get some answers. Judy indicated through grimaces, twisting and turning, and vocal kvetching that she wanted to get out of the hospital. She didn't like being hooked up to a machine—who would? And she didn't like the suction tube. As difficult as it was for me to hear this, I took it as a sign that she was improving. Don't many hospital patients begin to get a bit grumpy and want to go home as soon as they start feeling better?

I overheard the neurologist say that if Judy had no new seizures by the following day, she would be able to go back to a regular floor unit. At that point, as Judy started recovering and feeling better, she also started to kvetch more. I hoped that once she had the tubes removed and could be taken out of the bed for a change in position, the complaining would stop. But I was afraid that each day forward would bring the question of whether we had done right by her. Allowing the treatments, rather than seeking hospice, meant that we were prolonging her life. I continued to fear that her life would then consist not only of living at TNH but also of recurring hospital visits. My conundrum of wanting Judy to die but not wanting her to be dead continued.

Nurse Nadine confirmed that if Judy had no seizures that night, she'd be transferred back to a regular room and then, most likely in a week, she would be able to go back to TNH. When I told Judy this, she pouted and looked ready to cry. *Judy doesn't care if she's in CCU or a regular room. To her, there's no difference. She just doesn't want to go back to TNH. She wants to go home.* I imagined she would cry when she got there, and I wouldn't be able to go and sit there all day, every day as I'd been doing at the hospital. *There are benefits for her, being in the hospital.*

The next few days saw increased improvements, and Judy began to be pretty much back to normal in her responsiveness. She was still getting the nebulizer treatment, and that was still causing her to cough up mucus, which made her lips dry and cracked. Her food volume was increased and then reduced again, presumably because she wasn't tolerating the higher amount. One day she'd be alert and complaining; the next, though still responsive, she would be sleepier and complaining less. She seemed to be having stomach cramps and once woke up crying after a short nap.

Her oxygen level still went up and down, and while she had been put on nasal oxygen for a while, she then went back on the mask. *Herein lies a problem: The nursing staff is always changing. One nurse gets to know Judy and learns her patterns, and then a new nurse comes and looks at the numbers on the chart, not aware of Judy's patterns.* Nadine knew that if Judy's oxygen level went down to 90, it would come back up, so she was willing to wait before putting the mask on. However, a nurse who didn't know Judy thought she needed the mask.

With my head hanging low and shoulders sagging, I thought, *I guess it would be so much easier for everyone if Judy could talk.*

They were just waiting for a bed to send her back to a regular room. *I like it in the CCU. It's private and we don't have to deal with a room-mate. But Judy stopped seizing and her breathing is improved, so she really doesn't need the intensive care. We'll just have to deal with the change.*

David and my mom came to visit and keep me company when they could. Orin, Carrie, and my son Ilan came for a visit as well. Not long after they left on the day of their visit, Judy started to get fidgety and pouted as if she was going to cry. In general, it was hard to know the reason behind her tears. In the past, I would suggest different possibilities, and I'd often hit on the right one, and she would calm down. This time it seemed she was sad that her visitors had left. "Carrie and Orin had to go home to New Jersey. You remember how long it takes to get there." She pouted. "Remember how you didn't like the traffic when we used to go? How we had to tell the other drivers to hurry up and move out of the way?" She attempted to laugh through the mask. "They'll come back and visit again." That seemed satisfactory, and she made another laugh attempt and then fell asleep.

I'd been trying to deal with my mixed emotions about Judy getting better and returning to TNH. On the optimistic side, David said that maybe she'd be feeling better and therefore be happier. I knew that, in the end, I had no choice, and she would have to return to TNH. I consoled myself with the thought that it would still be at least a few more days until she left the hospital. First, she had to get to a regular room. I convinced myself that it was okay for her to return to TNH as long as she wasn't in pain and wasn't afraid and wasn't suffering. *I just have to close my eyes to the sadness she probably feels every day.*

When Judy finally got into a regular room, she was back on the nasal oxygen and seemed okay. I met the pulmonologist on my way in, and he said Judy was doing much better. He ordered another swallow evaluation to be done in the next couple of days. I was now ready for her to get out of the hospital. At that point, I felt that since she eventually would be going back to TNH, I preferred it be sooner rather than later. Her breathing seemed fine to me—I didn't hear any wheezing anymore. She had no fever, and the antiseizure medication was doing its job. I saw no reason for her to stay hospitalized once the feeding issue got resolved.

The feeding tube that had been inserted through her mouth into her stomach, however, became a bigger issue than I would have liked. When an aide came in to give Judy a wash-up, the tube came apart. I had feared that would happen because it seemed so unstable, and I had tried to convince myself that everyone there knew what they were doing, and it would be fine. I was wrong. It came out. And that meant that now they had to put it back in! They would have to take it out again to do the swallow evaluation and put it back in until the results came. The very first time they put it in, Judy had been unconscious, in the midst of a seizure. This time (and the next), I expected it would be awful. I wasn't allowed in the room while they did it, but I'd be able to imagine it. I told myself, *This happens to a lot of people. People get tubes. She'll survive!* The question became, *Will I?*

When they came to reinsert the tube, Judy had just fallen asleep. *It would be so nice if she would just stay sleeping while they put the tube in.* I waited outside her room. It was taking a long time. I didn't think it was going well. I heard her coughing and complaining. An LPN was putting it in under the RN's supervision. I got the feeling she hadn't done many of these procedures before. Finally, it was finished. They had switched the OG tube to a nasogastric tube (NG), this one going through her nose. She seemed very uncomfortable when I saw her, a sad look on her face. I tried to be positive. "Hey, Jude. I see they moved the tube. I think it's good that you don't have to have it in your mouth anymore." *Maybe it's better in the nose. It does make her look better, not to have anything sticking out of her mouth.*

Though my feelings about Judy being in TNH hadn't changed, I found myself actually looking forward to her being discharged from the hospital. I had resigned myself to the situation and was eager to get back to our routine. I had to return to work and would soon be unable to continue my daily visits to the hospital. Also, Judy's hospital roommate was schizophrenic and a real handful. She never stopped talking—mostly an imaginary conversation on the phone—and kept trying to get out of bed to go to the bathroom, even though she had a foley (catheter) and was hooked up to an IV. Every time she tried to get up, she was in danger of pulling one or both out. She was also unsteady on her feet and at risk of falling. An aide sat near her to make sure she didn't get up, but before I left there was a major scene because she got herself out of bed (on the other side from her foley and IV) and when the aide gently tried to put her back, the woman started yelling that the aide was abusing her. It was quite a scene, with other staff members coming in to help. Judy, who never liked arguments and yelling, got upset and started crying. They gave the woman something to calm her down, and I left there hoping there wouldn't be another scene during the night. The event was a sad reminder that there are people worse off than Judy.

A couple of days later, the doctor removed the oxygen completely, and Judy had her first taste of regular food. She still had the feeding tube through her nose, but they wanted to see if she would tolerate the food by mouth. If she was able to swallow the food without having a coughing fit, they'd then remove the nasal tube. The doctor said she would probably be discharged in a few more days. All that was great, but when I fed her dinner, she coughed—a lot. I didn't feed her very much because I was nervous about the coughing, and I figured she was still getting food through the tube, so she wouldn't be that hungry. I hoped that the coughing was because she hadn't eaten for a while or maybe because she felt the tube in her throat when she swallowed. I hoped the situation would improve, though I hadn't ruled out the need for a stomach tube. At that point, I had developed a wait-and-see attitude.

With Judy's improvement and nearing discharge from the hospital, my panic over her condition and my rush to look into hospice care started to feel foolish. In my defense, the doctors *did* indicate that she might not survive much longer. I'd truly believed that she would never recover to her "before" state and looked at hospice as an opportunity to end her suffering. I had to admit, though, that it had all seemed so much worse when she was sick and I thought she would never get better. Once she was almost back to her old self, I calmed down. I did not discount hospice completely, though, and thought it best to keep it in mind, should anything bad happen again. In the meantime, we were both getting bored at the hospital and I, at least, was looking forward to Judy getting back to TNH. Judy evidently did not feel the same, as she started crying when the doctor said she would be discharged soon and be taken back to the nursing home. She was clearly disappointed that she wasn't going *home*. I, of course, felt awful, but there was nothing that could be done about that. Just one more event over which I had absolutely no control.

Journal Entry
February 28, 2006

I want to write about my feelings, but suddenly I'm feeling self-conscious that this journal is so much about me and not really about Judy, though I tell myself that they are hopelessly intertwined. I'm so tired, I don't even want to think anymore. Everyone is rejoicing over the fact that Judy has improved so much—everyone but me. Of course, I'm thrilled that she is no longer sick. At the same time, though, I can't help thinking that if she had died, she would be at peace. I am also guiltily allowing myself to acknowledge the fact that I have something to gain by Judy dying, the freedom I lost six months ago. Of course, I will still have my mom to worry about, my children are not totally independent yet, and I still go to work. I would still have responsibilities, but I wouldn't have to gear myself up to go to TNH, wouldn't have to worry about feeding, walking, talking, or the length and frequency of my visits. The truth is that my life would be easier. It distresses me to think that I might want Judy to die because my life would then be easier. Yet, though I do question my motives, I will not accept that "ease" is what this is all about. Yes, it's a lot about me, but it comes from my concern for Judy. No, I won't have to worry, but what I won't be worrying about is Judy! Is she unhappy? Is she lonely? Do I visit often enough and long enough? Does she cry too often? Are her needs being met? Does she wish she could leave there? If she needs a feeding tube, will they be tending to it properly? Will she get other food to eat if she is able? Will something happen that will land her back in the hospital again, afraid and in pain? If something happens to me, will she ultimately be alone?

Yes, it would be easier for me if Judy were to die, but more importantly, maybe, is the question of whether it would also be better for her. What exactly does she have to live for? Occasional family visits? Is that worth it? I hardly think so. And other than her half-hour visits to the sensory room (and I'm assuming that Judy is brought there regularly, though I'm not at all sure), I honestly don't believe there is anything that she enjoys. So, as eager as I am for Judy to get out of the hospital, my feelings have not changed from the day the seizures began when I considered getting the hospice process going. I am disappointed that hospice is no longer an option, and I feel guilty that I didn't do what I believe to be best for my sister in the long term. There are those who might say, "Where there is life, there is hope," but I gave up hoping, as far as Judy is concerned, a long time ago. Sure, she might recover from an illness, but I have no reason to believe that her overall condition will ever change for the better. No, Judy is not in constant pain at TNH. No, it is not the worst place she could be. Yes, there are people who live in worse circumstances. But the fact that there are others who are worse off doesn't make it better for Judy.

14

It's Complicated

Judy is back at TNH. Just after four o'clock on March 1, the doctor came into Judy's hospital room and said she was being discharged—an ambulance would come for her in an hour. I was somewhat surprised at the quick decision, but I didn't argue and was relieved to be leaving the hospital. Judy, on the other hand, was yelling at the doctor and just about started crying after he left. I talked her out of it—"You're better now, Judy, and you don't need the hospital anymore." She calmed down. "When you go back to TNH, you'll get to see Erika again. She's probably thinking, *Hey, where did Judy disappear to? Did she get lost in the dining room or something?*" That got a laugh. She seemed okay, but I thought she was still hoping to go home—to her real home, the one before TNH, and that's why she was yelling at the doctor.

The ambulance showed up exactly an hour later. Judy wasn't ready. The nurse hadn't been told directly and hadn't yet looked at Judy's chart. There were still a few details to clear up and get finalized, so the ambulance left. The nurse had to call for another one. That one didn't come until 7:20, but we were all ready this time! We got to TNH at about 7:45, and Judy was relaxed, back in a now familiar place on her own bed with her own TV.

TNH was as if we had never left. I hoped they would get Judy back into her regular routine quickly. I hoped they would be careful feeding her and would stop the feeding if she started coughing, something I mentioned to the nurse. I hoped Judy wouldn't have another problem for a long time. I was prepared, though, if it didn't turn out to be very long at all. Only time would tell.

Being back at TNH turned out to cause somewhat of a relapse for me. Once again, the foul odors hit me as I walked out of the elevator onto the second floor. Once again, I recoiled at the sight of the residents sitting aimlessly in the hallway. It could be that I imagined it, but Judy seemed sadder. It was so much harder for me to get her to smile. Her eating concerned me as well. When I fed her, I did so slowly, waiting for her to swallow before I gave her more, watching for signs of a coming cough. The coughing did appear to be less severe, but she was gagging, and I half expected her to pass out from lack of air. As I watched her during the times we spent together, I wondered if she was angry at me for bringing her back to this place. The sadness that I saw in her face, her detached demeanor seemed more to indicate hopelessness, as if she'd finally given up on ever going home again. I found myself reflecting on my recent conflicting desires. I couldn't help thinking about how different things might have been had I opted for hospice. I awaited the warm weather of spring when we could once again walk outside. I hoped that maybe the walks would cheer us both.

They didn't. Eight months had now gone by since Judy was first brought to TNH. I'd love to be able to say that things were so much better, that everyone had fully adjusted and we were all happy. I'd love to be able to say that, but . . .

The good news is that during one of my visits, the nurse had come in to tell me that Judy had a new mattress that would better prevent bedsores and help heal her shoulder wound (yes, it was still there) and the sore on her hip. These were the kinds of things that led David and me to say that they were watching out for Judy and were taking care of her. But then, on one of David's weekend morning visits, he arrived at eleven, and Judy was still in her pajamas. She had a neck full of stuck-on cereal from breakfast. He made a big stink about it. They explained that they were short-staffed on the weekend. My reaction later, when David told me, was that I hadn't noticed any mass exodus of residents on weekends, and I wasn't aware that a person's needs lessened on Saturday and Sunday. At any rate, I wasn't surprised by the whole thing. In fact, when I was there during the week, I had noticed the same thing. Judy's mouth had been cleaned around the lips, but her neck was totally covered in dried-up cereal. I knew the difficulty of trying to keep food in Judy's mouth and how easily it dripped out. What upset me was that I arrived at TNH at nearly five in the afternoon, and her neck had been that way since breakfast! But I'm not David. I didn't make a stink. Maybe if I had, David wouldn't have had the same experience. Undoubtedly, I should have spoken up for my sister. Instead, I cleaned her up and made a mental note to bring wipes with me in the future. I did, however, ask the nurse to please make sure that Judy's nails got cut. They were always so long that I was afraid one would pierce her skin, as her hands were clenched shut all the time. In fact, I wondered how it hadn't happened yet, as this was not the first time that I'd asked for her nails to be clipped. On a subsequent trip, I came prepared with my own clippers. On one visit, I purposely left the nails long to see if I could rely on the nurse's assurance that they would monitor the situation. No surprises. I continued clipping. So, while we (meaning I) may not be our loved one's best advocates, we are their best caregivers. Even when we can no longer provide the care at home, it is up to us to continue to provide as much as we can wherever they are. How much better it would be, though, if we were both caregiver *and* advocate.

Judy and I celebrated (if that's really the word to use) our fifty-fourth birthday at TNH. On our way up to see Judy, David and I bumped into the administrator of the home. He asked us how things were going, commented on the scare we'd had with Judy two months earlier, and expressed thanks that she was now fully recovered. I didn't share the sentiment. Yes, it was good that she wasn't sick anymore, but was it so great that she continued living her sad TNH existence and that this was now where we had to celebrate birthdays?

I remembered the birthday parties my mother held for Judy and me when we were young. She would set up a table in the long hallway of our Bronx apartment, and our friends would come for cake and goodies. Candles were lit on the cake, Judy and I would make our wishes, then I would blow out the candles for both of us. We played games like pin the tail on the donkey, spinning around with a blindfold, our arms outstretched as we hoped to tape the donkey's tail in the appropriate place. Judy played too, with me spinning her chair around and holding her arm out to touch the spot where the tail would go, as she squealed with joy. Everyone had fun, and the sounds of laughter filled the apartment. Now, in TNH, David and I brought balloons, took Judy for a walk, and took some pictures; none of us enjoyed any of it. Judy didn't smile when she saw us or at any time during our visit. David commented later that she didn't seem happy at all. I couldn't remember when I had last heard her laugh. Indeed, the only emotional reaction she gave at all was when we brought her back and I said goodbye in the dining room, leaving her there to be fed. She vocalized a protest. I left her anyway.

Life at TNH seemed to be deteriorating. Erika's mother asked if we still needed the geri chair in the room, as it took up a lot of space. "They use it to take Judy to the sensory room, so she needs to have it here," I answered. Erika indicated that Judy no longer went to the sensory room. I said I would have to speak to Mary, and Erika's mom told me that Mary wasn't there anymore. "She left for another job." My heart sank, and my shoulders started to ache. Mary was the only one I could really talk to and who followed up. The nurse in charge confirmed that they hadn't been taking Judy to the sensory room since she got back from the hospital. That was over two months ago! "The orders are that Judy is only to be put in her chair for meals," the nurse informed me. I, in turn, informed her that Mary had said she should go to the sensory room in the geri chair. The nurse checked and told me that the geri chair was too big for Judy. My heart sank lower as I recalled feeling that the one positive Judy had at TNH was the sensory room. "It's important that Judy go, as she really enjoys it and it gives her something to do." The nurse said she would look into it and get back to me. She called me back later to tell me that they were getting a special cushion to put in a different geri chair that would be better for Judy. I wondered why they couldn't figure that out without me asking about it. The next time I went, Judy was "sitting" in the new chair, relaxing in the rec/dining room with her aide nearby. She looked comfortable. *How good it is when people listen to us. How important to remember to keep trying, however hopeless it may seem.*

I wanted to be able to cope with Judy's return to TNH but found that my tears fell all the way to TNH, were temporarily on hold during my visit, and resumed on my trip home. Though I thought I had reached the "acceptance" stage and could, robotically, just go where I had to go and do what I had to do and deal with it all, the hospital admission really did set me back. Every time I saw Judy's lack of emotion, every time I saw her condition worsening in any way—she was in the geri chair to eat her dinner one night, with a bandage on her foot covering a sore, and I couldn't take her outside for a walk because she'd had a slight fever earlier in the day—I thought of what might have been had the hospital outcome been different. I dreaded my visits because I knew I would be driving home in tears. David was considering cutting his visits to once a month because he found it too painful to see Judy so unhappy. He really couldn't bear the smell, and seeing the residents just standing or sitting around with nothing to do upset him. I couldn't blame him in the least for not wanting to go. I just thought that if he ever did stop visiting, it would be that much sadder for Judy.

I told David that I wanted to start looking around for a better place. I knew the IRAs that I had once hoped for were out of the question, but I thought that new facilities might have opened up that we didn't know about. I hoped that maybe I would find a place that was at least more inviting. *TNH is just so dreary and it smells so awful. It always amazes me that the staff is even as pleasant as they are.*

A couple of weeks later, Bobby's father died. I had put Judy on the bed and gone out into the hall to get a towel to put between her knees to keep them from becoming irritated by rubbing together, and Bobby called me over. Though he often called to me, asking me if I had anything to ask him, this time he called me over and told me, "My daddy died, and he's in heaven now."

I was a bit taken aback and answered that my daddy was in heaven too. He repeated what I said. That's what Bobby did—asked us to ask him questions, then repeated the question and gave an answer. Any response we made, he repeated. I said maybe my daddy and his daddy would meet in heaven. He didn't respond. In a clumsy attempt at offering condolences, I said, "I'm sorry to hear about your daddy. You must be very sad about it." He started to cry. Holding back my own tears, I lamely offered, "It's okay, because one day you will get to see your daddy again . . . when you go to heaven." He repeated what I said. I got my towel and went back to Judy.

When I left for home, about ten minutes later, Bobby called to me again. "When will I go to heaven?" This was very unusual—Bobby had never asked me a question before.

"You will go when it is time for you to go," I answered. He repeated it and then asked when that would be. "I don't know," I said. "Only G-d knows." He repeated it. His face puckered and his eyes got watery. I made an attempt at saying goodbye and wished for him to be happy. He repeated it and asked me how he could be happy. "Think a happy thought. Can you think of something happy?"

"Being with my mother makes me happy."

"How wonderful. Think that happy thought, and I'll see you next week." And with that, I left.

Two weeks after that, Rick died. Rick, who was probably in his sixties, lived diagonally across from Judy a couple of doors down from Bobby. When I heard he had died, my reaction was, *Good for him!* Then I thought about how old he was and how long he had lived the life he had. He was more abled than Judy, but he still lived at TNH. Good for Rick, and not good for Rick. I wondered if he would have said it was worth living as long as he did.

In reality, disabled people are no different from abled ones in that they experience a wide range of emotions, including sadness and joy. Many of us would say the disabled are given more than their fair share of challenges, yet even with those challenges, most find their lives worth living. In thinking more about it, I suppose Rick would have said it was worth it. He had made the best of what he was given. I wonder if sometimes it's harder for the loved ones. We want life to be good for those we love. There are those who accept the situation as it is and rejoice in the positives. And there are those, like me, who wish we can fix what has been broken. Yet just as the disabled are able to accept their condition, we, too, have no choice but to accept the limitations on how we can improve our loved ones' lives. We can only strive to do the best we can to help make their lives better.

Journal Entry
August 29, 2006

One year. In some ways it seems like yesterday, and in others it was a lifetime ago. I feel I have come far, and yet nothing has changed. I don't cry every day, but the tears still come. I am more comfortable with the nursing home environment, but I still hold my breath as I exit the elevator onto the second floor. Currently, I enjoy my visits with Judy, but I continue to wish I didn't have to go.

Last night at about eleven o'clock, we received a phone call telling us that Judy was running a fever. My immediate reaction was not of concern for her but of hope for my future—and I say that deliberately, my future. For, in the span of the year, I have come to accept that I do not have an answer as to whether Judy's current life is worth living; I only know that my life would be easier if she were to die. And if that makes me an awful person, then so be it.

It was at the moment when I learned that they had readmitted Judy to the hospital this morning that I started thinking I can no longer do this. I have no more of myself to give. I called to make sure she was not crying, and I remained at my job with no intention of rushing over there, hoping that because the hospital situation was no longer new to her, she would not be so scared. At least it's a fever and not her breathing. She will be there for several days—enough for her to get the antibiotics that they are giving her intravenously. Because of work, I cannot be there all day as I was last time. Or maybe it's just that I no longer have the energy. One year. Some things change, and some things remain the same. Guilt is one that seems to remain always.

Judy was unresponsive when I visited her in the hospital. She didn't seem to care about what was going on around her and just lay emotionless in her bed. I'm not complaining. I prefer it this way. I think it eases my guilt to think that when I'm not there with her, she doesn't really notice. I try to believe that she has developed a tolerance, that she just goes along with the changes: new people, new place. I don't really believe it, but I try to convince myself.

The seizures are back. Short ones. The nurse says it's because of the fever. They changed her medication and that should help. Her fever is down from 103.5 to 101.6. She'll probably be able to go home—no, I keep correcting David on that, and yet I make the same mistake—she'll probably be able to go back to TNH on Friday. It makes no difference to me right now, though when she starts feeling better and gets nudgy about being in the hospital, I'll probably feel differently.

When I got home after my visit, my guardianship papers were in the mail. I now officially have the authority to make health-care decisions for Judy. Interesting timing. I would give it up in a heartbeat, though, if I didn't feel it was necessary for me to be prepared to make those decisions; if I didn't feel that, without the ability to do so, Judy's sad life might continue indefinitely.

There are those who might say that I want Judy to die, and even I have said as much in my wish to relieve her of suffering, but it is really much more complicated than that. What I really wish is to be able to look back on my childhood and remember the times that Judy and I intentionally dressed in the same clothing and had the same hairstyle so no one would be able to tell us apart—like the two little girls who lived across the street on Davidson Avenue. What I really wish is to have a memory of how we danced, not by me twirling her around in my arms but hand in hand, and feet to feet. What I really wish is to reminisce about our shared conversations—private conversations that only sisters can share. But those memories can never be. That world never existed for us.

So instead, I wish for the future, and it is for Judy to live in a happy place, a pretty place where sunshine comes through the windows and flowers bloom everywhere. A place where people not only take care of her but love her—with time and interest to ask her what she wants and listen to her cryptic replies. I want Judy to be special to those who care for her. But that, too,

    will never be.

Returning to more realistic yearnings, what I wish for the present is to see Judy smile. I want to know that she is happy. I want to know there is more joy in her life than our twice-a-week family visits. I want to know that, in fact, those visits bring her joy. But those realities, as well, do not exist.

Finally, what I want is for Judy to tell me what it is that she wants. Even that is out of my reach.

And so, since what I do want can never be, I will tell you what I do not want. I do not want Judy to suffer, and I see her suffering every day. I do not want her languishing in her bed because she can no longer sit in the wheelchair or even the geri chair. I do not want the never-ending battle with body sores. I do not want the recurring hospital admissions. I do not want her lying in a hospital bed for weeks at a time with tubes and IVs and breathing masks. I do not want to be told repeatedly that they're trying a new medication today because the seizures are back.

The bottom line is that what I want, what I desperately wish, is for Judy to be at peace. I do not want her to die, but I do not want to prolong what I see as her suffering. And though, in the end, we may arrive at the same place—death—there is a difference.

15

The Pendulum Comes to a Halt

Brought on by the fever, Judy's hospital stay, which I expected to be only a few days, turned out to last six weeks. It took that long for the doctors to get her seizures under control. During that time, they once again inserted a nasal feeding tube. "The tube is only a temporary solution to the issue of giving Judy nutrition," the doctor explained. "We would like to insert a feeding tube directly to her stomach. We need your consent."

Déjà vu. My head started swirling as thoughts of prolonging a life that contained very little, if any, quality filled my brain.

"No," I responded.

"Would you like to make an application for hospice?"

"Yes."

I didn't call my mother. I didn't call my brothers. I didn't ask David. I made the decision and felt secure that I was doing the right thing for Judy and that my family would agree.

During her hospital stay, Judy's bedsores got worse—there was one on her hip that was particularly bad. The doctor wanted to have it cleaned, but it required a surgical procedure that wasn't allowed on hospice—no curative measures. I cringed when I saw the wound and felt stabbed in the heart when I thought that it would not be treated because of my decision for hospice. I imagined it must have been painful, and I wasn't confident that she was getting sufficient pain medication. I was still trying to come to grips with this new development, only mildly relieved that the doctors said they would try to clean the wound as best as possible without the surgery, when—after six weeks of hospitalization—I received a call from TNH saying that Judy would be returning that evening.

I was so stunned, I gasped. *What do they mean, Judy's going back to TNH? I've been visiting her every day at the hospital, speaking with doctors and nurses, and no one has mentioned that Judy would be going back to TNH, no less that her return would be imminent.* My hands were shaking as I called the hospital. The person I spoke to didn't know anything about the transfer. Finally, after speaking to several different people, I was told that TNH was beginning a hospice care program and that Judy would be accepted into hospice there. They would allow a feeding tube—in fact, they wouldn't let her return without one. Once again my brain filled up with so many thoughts that I was afraid it would forget to tell my lungs to breathe. *Take it easy. Judy will never be able to leave TNH, but at least she'll be on hospice. They're not taking that away.* My brain continued filling up. *What will her life look like on hospice at TNH? How can I send her back with an NG tube? It must be extremely uncomfortable. I can't imagine having that thing up my nose and down the back of my throat all day, every day. And how will they be able to care for her with a tube going through her nose? How will she shower? How will I take her for walks?*

I went over everything in my mind, took a deep breath, and told the doctor that if they were going to send her back with a feeding tube, they may as well put in the G (stomach) tube. It would be much more comfortable, and the food would only be connected at night. The next day, the doctors did the procedure and took the opportunity to surgically clean her wound. The ache in my shoulders eased when I heard that. The following day, Judy went back to TNH. Despite the procedure to clean her worst wound, she returned with other awful bedsores and, because of these sores, she was no longer expected to ever be able to sit in a wheelchair. The new seating mold (that was still being made) became a non-issue, and the geri chair became Judy's escape from her bed. Going for walks outside was a thing of the past.

*

Though I had thought about hospice from the moment it was first brought up to me, I had wavered on whether or not it was the right thing to do. As I learned, the mere *idea* of hospice can be difficult to accept. It means acknowledging, on some level, that your loved one is going to die. And yet it is a most compassionate gift to give to that special person. The main responsibility of the hospice nurse is to make sure the patient is comfortable and not in too much pain. For the loved ones, this is extremely comforting. I felt more than just comfort, however. As the summer ended and the fall season progressed, I thought of how hospice was saving my sanity. Our hospice nurse, Eva, became my emotional support, and I relied on her for information about Judy's condition and care and to relay my concerns to the staff. As part of hospice, Judy was given a part-time aide. Lorna was special. She asked us questions so she could better understand Judy, and she talked to Judy and caressed her when she felt Judy needed comforting. As I continued visiting Judy, my shoulders, my heart, my whole body was so much more relaxed knowing that Lorna was there at least part of the time that I couldn't be. It calmed me to know that Judy wasn't alone, that someone was with her, talking to her and watching over her.

When they brought Judy back to TNH following the hospital visit, now on hospice, she was placed in a room on the first floor. This was a major plus for David and me. We no longer had to go up to the malodorous second floor with its depressing long, narrow hallways lined with wheelchairs. The first floor had mostly non-CP patients who were there for rehab and, because it was off the lobby, it was much brighter. The tightness I felt in my body every time I began my journey to visit eased up a bit. Of course, being on a new floor meant leaving Erika, and we felt sad about that. Instead, there began a series of different roommates, some more tolerable for us than others. None ever engaged in conversation with us when we visited or seemed to take any interest in Judy. Each time a roommate left, we would pray another wouldn't come—it was so quiet and peaceful when Judy was alone in the room. Alas, to our great disappointment, they always did come.

Then, at eleven o'clock one night late in December, I was awakened by a phone call from TNH to say that Judy was running a fever of 105 and her breathing had become very labored. "Her condition is very serious. We don't think she'll make it through the night." Because Judy was on hospice, and I had given prior instructions that she not be hospitalized for any reason, TNH could not call an ambulance. I quickly dressed and rushed over, not knowing quite what to expect but understanding that if I didn't get there soon, I might never see my sister alive again. When I arrived, she was in her bed, half-asleep, struggling to breathe. I got a chair and put it as close to her as I could get. I sat with her all night, rubbing her arm and listening to her Cheyne-Stokes breathing—breathing that gradually decreases to a complete stop and then returns to normal—afraid at every moment that each breath might be her last and the next one might not come. One might think, after all my wishing and praying, that I would be glad for this moment. That I would sit by Judy's side, hoping for that last breath. But it wasn't so. Sometimes when our wish is about to come true, we suddenly realize it's not what we had thought it would be. I simply wasn't ready for my death wish to come true, and I realized that I might never be.

It was a huge surprise to all of us that, though no one thought Judy would survive the night, she recovered suddenly at about six in the morning. I had fallen asleep and awoke to find that Judy's breathing was much softer and her fever was down. She looked at me sitting by her bed with an expression that said, *What in the world are you doing here at this hour?* By the next day, it was as if the episode had never happened.

The rest of December and January continued without incident, but at the end of February, on one of my visits, I spotted a very small seizure—almost unnoticeable except for the blinking of her eyes. I pointed it out to the nurse, and she noted it in Judy's records. That episode didn't last long, but I noticed a couple more every so often, still so mild that I wasn't even sure at first. Then, in mid-March, the seizures started coming regularly, still mild but more obvious and more often. They were back and, this time, they never left, gradually lengthening in frequency and duration.

Surprisingly, in the middle of April, I was told that hospice was planning to discharge Judy because her condition had become "stable." My heart racing, tears flowing, and barely able to speak due to my sobs, I immediately called Eva. She said she would make a call to find out what was going on and that I shouldn't worry. She assured me that she could get a continuance. Before anything could even happen, though, Judy developed another fever. A short time after that, Eva called to say that Judy's hospice status had been reinstated. Now the tears that flowed from my eyes were those of relief and gratitude. I don't know what I would have done if they had taken Judy off hospice, if they had taken away her aide, and if they were once again allowed to take her to the hospital when they felt it was needed, despite my instructions otherwise. Among the fears that ran through my head at the time was that of Judy being placed back on the second floor. That, by itself, seemed too much to bear.

Hospice was reinstated, but all was not well. Judy's seizures, mainly visible by her eyes veering up and off to the left accompanied by continuous eyelid flutters, continued to get longer. In fact, they eventually became almost nonstop, each lasting several minutes with only a few seconds in between. She was no longer responsive, and I couldn't even be sure if she was aware that she was seizing.

I thought back to a day a couple of months earlier when David and I had visited together. Judy was sitting in the geri chair in the hall. It was lunchtime at the time of our visit. Because she received her feedings through her G-tube overnight, she didn't need to be fed. As we watched the trays of food being brought into the dining room for the other residents, David spotted cups of ice cream. He asked Judy if she would like some. We thought we saw a small jaw drop *yes*. "Even though Judy is getting nutrition through the tube, it would be nice for her to feel food in her mouth and on her lips," he asserted. We weren't supposed to be giving Judy any food, but we didn't think a little bit of soft ice cream could do any harm; rather, it might give her pleasure. David grabbed an ice cream cup and spoon and brought it back. I gave Judy a taste. She opened her mouth for it, but it was as if she had forgotten what to do with it once it got inside. Her tongue didn't work at pushing it down, and her mouth pretty much stayed motionless. I tried a couple of spoonfuls, but the ice cream ended up on her bib, and I gave up. She didn't complain when I stopped, and I thought that she didn't really care. I thought, *It doesn't matter that she didn't swallow it. At least she had an opportunity to taste and feel coolness in her mouth.* I could only hope it was somewhat pleasing for her, but even of that, I couldn't be sure.

Back in the present, the memory receded, and the point was brought home to me that when situations change for the worse, past difficult times can suddenly seem not so terrible after all. It's just that we don't know that things will worsen when a situation is bad, so we tend to think they're already as bad as they can be. Perhaps if I could have accepted the difficult situations and done the best I could with them instead of harping on the hardship they brought, I would have been able to get through them more easily.

David, Mom, and I continued visiting Judy as often as we could, though I wasn't even sure she knew we were there. As we talked to her through her seizures, I wondered if she could hear us. How draining it was to watch her like that, not knowing if she was in pain or discomfort as she floated from one seizure to the next. I longed to tell her a story and hear her laughing response. That laughter, the main positive indication of the quality of her life, was a thing of the past. Where was her quality of life now?

It was at that point that I decided Judy had had enough, and I was ready to take action. I wrote a letter to Dr. Z, Judy's TNH doctor, asking that the G-tube be removed so that Judy could be allowed to die. In response, an administrator at TNH called me in to speak to him during one of my visits. "We spoke to Dr. Z, and we are not going to allow Judy's feeding to stop. It would cause her death, and we cannot knowingly do that." They tried to dissuade me by explaining that death from starvation is slow, very unpleasant, even painful, and not at all peaceful. I, of course, didn't want Judy to suffer, but my thinking was that either she was already suffering or she didn't know what was going on and wouldn't know she wasn't getting food. In either case, I figured she could receive medication to alleviate any pain she might have. I tried to argue my case, but the result was the same. They wouldn't do it.

I spoke to Eva about it and her suggestion was, "If you really want to stop the feeding and end Judy's life, you could take her out of TNH and bring her to stay at your house. There, you would be free to remove the tube. Judy would remain on hospice and continue to receive palliative care."

I hesitated. That was a huge step. Not only would it mean that I would need to find a place where Judy could stay comfortably in my home but that I would absolutely be the one responsible for her death. It meant either getting my mother's consent or, more likely, having to go against Mom's wishes because I knew she would never agree to hastening Judy's death. It meant that David and I would be watching her slowly die. I wasn't sure that I could do any of that. David *was* sure. He said no.

And then, just a few weeks after the near hospice-ending incident, it happened. Despite the endless hours of my wishing, hoping, and praying, I was shocked when I got the news. On May 11, as I sat in staff development at work, a distressed message came over the intercom: "Excuse me. Debbie Morris, you have a phone call. It's very important." A sense of urgency came through in the secretary's voice. I put down my pen, stood up, and calmly left the room. Once outside the room, I quickened my pace and then broke out into a run as I made my way down the long hallway to the main office. Panic raced through my body. *Could it be about Judy? What if it's one of my kids?* I remember Wendy's eyes, full of compassion, as I entered the main office and she pointed to the phone. My heart was racing and I could hardly breathe as I reached for it, trying to calm myself by thinking of the likelihood that it was TNH calling to tell me that Judy had a fever. My hands shook as I lifted the receiver and searched for the correct button to push. David's voice came through softly from the other end of the line with just two simple words. "Judy died." My heart stopped and, as I began to absorb his words, all I could think of was, *I have to get out of here. I have to go. I have to be with her.* In another moment I was off the phone, fleeing to the privacy of my office. And there, I sat at my desk and sobbed.

The shock of the news sent horrific thoughts to my head. *Why am I crying? Is it because my sister, my twin, my literal other half has just died, or is it relief that it's over, that my wish has come true and this horrible nightmare is at an end?* That question in itself was torturous, and I forced it out of my mind. I calmed down with the help of friends who had arrived from the staff development room, sensing that something was terribly wrong. "I have to go," I said, as I told them the news. Fran asked if she could drive me, but I needed to be alone, and as I continued to take in breaths, I felt more in control. I left school in a state of disbelief.

I drove to TNH, where I met David and my mother. Judy was in her bed, the curtain drawn all around her. Her body was there, pale, except where her skin was beginning to turn purple, and had already turned cold. Her body was there, but she had clearly left. Maybe she was hovering nearby. We spoke to her, said our goodbyes, and softly kissed her cheek. "You're in a good place, now, Jude. You'll see Daddy and you can hang out with him, and one day we'll all be together again. And we'll have lots of stories to tell each other. So bye for now. Tell Daddy we say hi. We love you very much!" My biggest disappointment was that her body was as before, her arms bent up at the elbows, her fists tightly turned inward. I had hoped that, in death, Judy's spasticity would disappear and that her body would, at last, be at peace.

A day later, I was still in a state of disbelief. It had been a long, very difficult series of events leading up to this day, and I felt a deep sadness mixed with a sense of relief, as if a terrible weight had been lifted from my shoulders. I'd worried about her for so long. I never asked about the actual cause of death. I didn't know if she was alone when she died or if someone was with her. What I did know was that she was no longer suffering.

As I thought about the events leading up to Judy's death, I remembered how I would leave her after each of my visits following the onset of the persistent seizures. Never sure if she even heard me, I would give her a kiss and whisper, "Jude, it's okay if you want to go. You don't have to stay here anymore. It's okay. We'll be okay." On the evening before she died, I had reached my tolerance limit for seeing her the way she was. I got up to leave, kissed her on her cheek, and very firmly said just two words, "It's time." And I turned and left. I still believe today that my message got through and it was my unwavering determination in my last words to her that allowed her to finally let go.

Journal Entry
May 17, 2007

Several days have passed. I am calm. I can talk about Judy without tears. I know that she is in a better place. I know that she is no longer suffering. I saw in her, in the funeral parlor as the cloth was unwrapped from around her face so I could view her, an undeniable peacefulness. That's when I knew—she is okay. That is how I hope I will remember her at the end.

The funeral was simple, a graveside service with the immediate family and a few close relatives. I read a eulogy I had written, containing a reference to a Yiddish song our father used to sing to Judy and me when we were small to help Judy fall asleep. My brother David, remembering the words, sang it after we said Kaddish. It was so beautiful, his singing, filling me with a deep sense of peace. Remembering the happy times of Judy's life with those who loved her, the knowledge that her suffering was no longer, I felt the healing begin.

May 25, 2007

I find myself relieved but missing her. I miss going to see her, even though I dreamed of no longer having that obligation. I feel less than whole, as a part of me is missing, and I am saddened by the thought that we will never share another birthday.

In the weeks before Judy's death, I found myself becoming more and more depressed. Our earlier attempts at giving Judy ice cream or pudding—just to give her some sense of eating pleasure—were met mostly with an inability to swallow. Her increasing lack of response to us was anguish for me. She seemed so sad, like everything good in her life had been stripped away and she was left with no hope. The surprise of her death caused me to focus on more immediate demands—whom to notify, funeral arrangements, shiva (the Jewish ritual of seven days of mourning following the death of a close relative or spouse). The shiva was helpful, and I found the support I received to be extremely comforting. Then it was back to work and routine. I was busy. Now the sadness has returned.

I want to grieve the loss of my sister, but I am not comfortable with my grief. I miss her but wonder, What exactly am I missing? I cannot mourn the loss of our sisterly conversations, for there were none. I cannot mourn that we no longer share experiences, going out to movies or dinner or for walks on the beach. I miss sharing secrets, having her as a confidante. But I always missed that. So what is different now? Why am I so sad? I think I miss having a sister. I always thought of Judy as being my other half, so now there is an emptiness in her place. I think I also miss the good things we once had that are now forever beyond our reach. For even though our childhood joys were left in the past, and the dreams I dreamed did not exist in reality, there was a piece of me that in some fantastical way always believed it could yet happen. And now it most definitely cannot. Not in life, anyway. With Judy's death, so died the possibility of magic.

June 15, 2007

It's been five weeks since Judy's death. I feel myself healing, and I'm okay with that. At first I resisted, afraid of letting go, afraid of seeing myself as callous. But the healing feels good, so I accept it. After-work hours have taken on a new routine—and they do not include trips to TNH. On my way home from a busy day at work, I think less often of my life of just a few weeks ago. No longer is my first thought about Judy one of her lying in her bed so sick that I have to force myself to think of her at other times. My thoughts are more peaceful now. The picture in my mind of Judy in her final days has been replaced by the Judy in a photo that I've kept on my desk at work and at home: Judy, smiling in her wheelchair in our house, in earlier and better times.

I will miss the drive down the parkway with its bloom of color in autumn, its deserted yet ever-so-peaceful dark evenings of winter. I will miss the spring and summer walks over the bridge with Judy. But I will never miss walking through the doors of TNH, my body tensing, holding my breath, anticipating what I would find when I got down the hall. I will not miss the sadness that is inherent in such a place.

At the moment, I find myself more accepting of the guilt that will always be with me. Yes, I could have been a better sister over the years, but the truth is that I didn't think she needed me as much then. After I moved from our apartment building, there were weekly visits with David and my children for Friday night Shabbat dinner. There were walks with Judy and my mother to a garden and visits to our house. Yes, I could have visited the apartment more often, spending time with Judy in her own home when transporting her by car became more difficult. But all that I could have done but didn't is in the past, and I am now able to leave it there. In the more recent years, when her care at home started to deteriorate, I looked away. I didn't want to see. Again, I could have done better, much better, but that, too, is in the past. I look now at the final year and nine months, and although I will always be sorry for Judy's suffering, I am comfortable in the choices I made. I was there for Judy in the only way I knew to be; there was no more I could have done.

I will forever be sorry that things couldn't have been different for all the years of our lives, but I will also forever be grateful for having Judy in my life. As the pain of the last year and nine months fades, its place will hopefully be filled with memories of the laughter and the happy times we shared together. Though I find it so hard to say goodbye, I know she will always be in my heart.

Epilogue
Finding Peace

Grief is an extraordinary phenomenon. It is ever changing as we go through it. After Judy's death, I continually looked for signs that I was *getting better*. The initial shock of her death threw me for a loop. After even a short time passed, however, I began to accept that she was no longer here. In July of that year, I wrote a letter to Dr. M: "I am much better now. . . . I can now think of Judy in happier times." When I recently found that letter, I was surprised to see that it wasn't what I remembered it to be. I had been angry at Dr. M for forcing my family to put Judy into a nursing home. I remember wanting to write:

You said that Judy would not survive for more than two years if she wasn't placed. Well, look what happened. We took her out of the only home she knew and put her in a strange place with people she didn't know, unable to communicate other than by crying, and for what? She didn't even last those two years! She could have continued living at home, without the trauma of the move, and she would have died in peace. We caused her suffering for no good reason.

That's what I had wanted to write at the time and what I thought I had written as I opened the letter now. I was surprised to see that it wasn't that at all. Instead, it was a letter thanking Dr. M for all he had done for Judy—keeping in contact with the doctor at TNH, consulting with her on the issue of Judy's feeding, and monitoring Judy's progress. I remember now that despite my anger, I couldn't bring myself to send him those angry words. I must have recognized that anger serves no good purpose. It eats away at us and can cause us to become bitter.

Instead, I chose to look for the good. I was able to recognize that, although I had fought placing Judy and had felt forced into doing so, he had threatened to report Judy to Adult Protective Services because he cared. He could not know the future any more than I could. He could not have foreseen that Judy would end up with seizures brought on by asthma medication. He could not have known how terrible her end would actually be. I invited Dr. M to respond to my letter to help me better understand what had happened at the end. I'm sorry that I never received a response.

I tried to find comfort in the idea that it was G-d's plan for Judy to go into the home. I told myself that maybe it was easier for my mother that way. Though forced to separate, Mom adjusted to her new reality, and when Judy died, the final separation was not as stark. Perhaps due to the trauma of separation, Mom had lost her concept of time, and she believed it had been years since Judy lived with her, that the room down the short hallway from hers had long been empty. After tears were shed, the only difference in my mother's life was that instead of visiting Judy on the weekend, she came to visit with me.

Years earlier, in one of our rare emotional talks on the subject of placing Judy in a home, Mom had told me her belief that Judy would not live very long in such a situation. I thought it was her way of coping with the inevitability of placement—it was better to think that Judy would not have to suffer for long. The irony is that Dr. M's argument for placing Judy was that she would not live more than two years in her home situation. Instead, it turned out that my mother was right.

I have since learned that TNH has become a rehabilitation center and is no longer a nursing home. The residents who lived in the home when Judy was there found placement elsewhere. It gives me comfort to think that their lives are better for it.

When I first decided to put my journal and my memories into a book, not long after Judy's death, I could read no further than the first couple of journal entries before I had to stop, my vision distorted by the tears falling from my eyes, my lungs gasping for air as sobs emanated from my body. I tried again periodically over the next number of years, never able to get much further. In fact, the tears continue to flow as I now remember the last months of my sister's life.

I think back now to how, after a year had gone by, I realized that although I had thought I was "better" after only two months, my grief had not ended quite so soon. At the one-year mark, I recognized the depression I had been feeling, how any joy that I felt was diminished somewhat by sadness. Another year passed, and I again thought I was finally "over it," until a year after that when I once again looked back and realized it had not yet ended. Though each year was a little lighter than the previous one, I continued to grieve for my sister for a very long time. The physical pain from the permanent hole in my heart lessened, but the guilt remained as strong as ever. I truly believed that I, and I alone, could have prevented those final months. I, and I alone, had allowed her to be placed. I, and I alone, should have fought harder for her.

Carrie recognized my grief and suggested that I seek counseling. I remember my stubbornness in thinking that it couldn't possibly help. How could anyone understand what I had gone through? How could someone help me if they hadn't had my experience? It took a second heartbreak to show me how wrong I was. The illness and ultimate death of my husband, David, which came nine years after Judy's, made my life so unbearable that I knew I wouldn't be able to do it alone.

Everyone experiences grief differently, and there is no right way to get through it. For me, the counseling I sought and received after David's death gave me the opportunity to tell this story. Therapy showed me that it didn't matter that the listener had not walked in my shoes. What mattered was that she listened. I never wanted to burden my friends or family with my heartbreak and so had kept it all inside following Judy's death. After David died, counseling gave me the outlet to pour out what was in my heart; it allowed me to sort out my feelings, to release some of the sadness so it didn't get locked up inside me, and to ultimately accept that David was never coming back. In the process of healing following David's death, I was also able to talk about Judy. With the help of Dr. E, I was finally able to accept the impact that Judy had on my life and to overcome the pain and guilt I had felt throughout our lives and especially the last year and nine months of hers. I will never know if counseling following Judy's death would have gotten me to that point sooner. Perhaps I just wasn't ready at that time. I think I will always wish I could have done it differently with Judy, that maybe there was a way I could have kept her from the experience of TNH. But the fact is, I didn't. And if there is one thing I have learned from David's death, it's that there is no going back. We cannot change what has already happened. We can only accept it, rejoice in what we had that was good, and continue to move forward.

Judy, I'm sorry the end was so difficult. I know, though, that you are in a good place. And I believe that one day we will be together again. Then we will have that long overdue conversation and we will have that loving embrace for which I ache, and together we will laugh as we spin around in our dance, hand in hand, as it was always meant to be.

Acknowledgments

Let me begin by first thanking the people who made this publication possible: my publisher, Brooke Warner, at She Writes Press, for the incredible support she gives her authors and for all her work in getting my story out to the public; Shannon Green, my project manager, for her expert guidance through the publishing process and for her quick, ever-patient, always cheerful responses to my many questions; Caitlin Hamilton Summie CH Marketing and Publicity, for her tireless diligence, advice, and understanding of my shy nature; and to Caitlin and Rick Summie for their expert help in getting the word out; Barrett Briske, for doing an amazing job researching the copyright information I needed; Jennifer Caven, for her first-rate copy editing; Katie Caruana for spot-on proofreading; Libby Jordan for getting me started on social media; Maggie Ruf for setting up an amazing website; and a very special thank-you to Annie Tucker, without whom this project would never have made it to book form. Thank you, Annie, for your expert coaching, your constant encouragement, and your wise insights. You taught me so much about memoir writing and gave me reason to believe in myself. I also want to give a special thanks to my partner, Robert Lande, for his invaluable input and support throughout the final stages of my writing.

When I first began writing about Judy, it was with the purpose of letting friends and family know what was going on. Sending one email to everyone meant not having to be on the phone for countless hours, bringing up raw emotions again and again. I quickly found my writings to be therapeutic, and thus, my journal began. I thank each of my email recipients for wanting to hear what I had to say, for encouraging me to continue my writings, and for their heartfelt responses. They helped me through a most difficult time in my life, and I am forever grateful. They are (in alphabetical order): my brothers and sisters-in-law, David and Reida Chein and Orin and Carrie Chein; and friends Teri Fields, Ann Hurwitz, Fran Katz, Jane Schlanger, Judith Schutzman, and Alice Talmud.

I especially thank Fran Katz, who accompanied me to TNH on numerous occasions, making those trips so much more bearable; Jane Schlanger for the idea that I could turn my journal into a book, and for running out to purchase nightgowns for Judy at a moment's notice; Teri Fields for her continuous expression of concern and for converting some of those nightgowns from long-sleeved into short; Judith Schutzman for always checking in, making sure I was okay; Alice Talmud for always knowing just the right thing to say and for doing my final read-through; school social worker Gila Calev for giving me a place to cry; and my brothers and sisters-in-law for allowing me to take the lead, even though I didn't always think I wanted it.

Thank you to the staff at TNH for continuing each day to help and care for so many people who could not care for themselves. You are amazing! In particular, I would like to thank Judy's floor nurses, Ingrid and James; her aide Hyacinth; and her aide Guerlande, who lovingly began taking Judy outside for walks when I couldn't be there, until it was no longer possible. A very special thank-you to nurse Diane, who showed me how she read Judy's eyes, and who gave Judy such special care and attention. Thank you to Eva from Hospice of New York for the extraordinary support she gave me, and to hospice aide Lorna for her compassion and care.

I am forever grateful to my parents, Norma and Dr. Isidor Chein, for keeping Judy at home at a time when common practice was to institutionalize, thereby allowing us to be a complete family and allowing me to have my twin sister close in my life, and to my grand-mother Sarah Cohen for being an integral part of making all that possible.

Thank you to my children for reminding me of the normalities of living when I was so stressed out. Guiding your journey into adult-hood allowed me to keep a foothold in our family life.

There are not enough thanks that I can give to my husband David. When I used to try to thank you for going to Judy on days that I could not bring myself to go, you would tell me you didn't want thanks—you were doing it for Judy. But I do thank you. I thank you for all you did for my family over the years since your arrival from Israel. And I thank you for your endless support in those last difficult months, for tirelessly being there when we needed you, for your sensitivity and caring, and for always trying so hard to make life better for Judy. Know how special you were to her.

Finally, a very special thank-you to Judy, for always being my pal, for putting up with my silly humor, for being my game partner through our growing-up years, and for enjoying the walks we took together even after we had grown. Most of all, thank you, Judy, for teaching me about love and the joy that comes from making someone laugh.

About the Author

photo credit: Jamie Kilgore Photography

Born in the Bronx, New York, Ms. Morris lived on Long Island (Plainview) for most of her adult life. The youngest (by five minutes) of four children, family has always been important to her. Married for forty-four years and since widowed, she is mother to three wonderful sons, two amazing daughters-in-law, and an adorable granddaughter. Ms. Morris worked in the field of early childhood education, receiving master's degrees from Queens College, Hofstra University, and Bank Street College of Education. Her work included classroom teacher to preschool and kindergarten children and reading teacher to kindergartners needing extra support. Ms. Morris is retired and loves to take walks in nature, solve *New York Times* crossword puzzles, and knit blankets for charity. She currently resides in Mount Kisco, New York, with her new partner.

SELECTED TITLES FROM SHE WRITES PRESS

She Writes Press is an independent publishing company founded to serve women writers everywhere. Visit us at www.shewritespress.com.

Edna's Gift: How My Broken Sister Taught Me to Be Whole by Susan Rudnick. $16.95, 978-1-63152-515-5

When they were young, Susan and Edna, children of Holocaust refugee parents, were inseparable. But as they grew up and Edna's physical and mental challenges altered the ways she could develop, a gulf formed between them. Here, Rudnick shares how her maddening—yet endearing—sister became her greatest life teacher.

No Spring Chicken: Stories and Advice from a Wild Handicapper on Aging and Disability by Francine Falk-Allen. $16.95, 978-1-64742-120-5

A companion to Falk-Allen's memoir *Not a Poster Child*, this handbook deftly and humorously shares tips and stories about disability-oriented travel, how to "be with" and adapt to a handicapped or aging person, and simple assistive health care we can employ in order to live our best and longest lives.

Not a Poster Child: Living Well with a Disability—A Memoir by Francine Falk-Allen. $16.95, 978-1631523915

Francine Falk-Allen was only three years old when she contracted polio and temporarily lost the ability to stand and walk. Here, she tells the story of how a toddler learned grown-up lessons too soon; a schoolgirl tried her best to be a "normie," on into young adulthood; and a woman finally found her balance, physically and spiritually.

Loving Lindsey: Raising a Daughter with Special Needs by Linda Atwell. $16.95, 978-1631522802

A mother's memoir about the complicated relationship between herself and her strong-willed daughter, Lindsey—a high-functioning young adult with intellectual disabilities.

A Leg to Stand On: An Amputee's Walk into Motherhood by Colleen Haggerty. $16.95, 978-1-63152-923-8

Haggerty's candid story of how she overcame the pain of losing a leg at seventeen—and of terminating two pregnancies as a young woman—and went on to become a mother, despite her fears.